Creating Connections:
Celebrating the power of groups

Creating Connections:

Celebrating the power of groups

Edited by

Lucia Berman-Rossi
Marcia B. Cohen
Holly Fischer-Engel
Editors

w&b

MMX

© Whiting & Birch Ltd 2010
Published by Whiting & Birch Ltd,
Forest Hill, London SE23 3HZ

ISBN 9781861771216

Printed in England and the United States by Lightning Source

Contents

Acknowledgements

We thank the following for their hard work and support which contributed to making the 25th Anniversary Symposium of AASWG a success:

Planning Committee for the 25th Annual International Symposium of the Association for the Advancement of Social Work with Groups, Inc., October 16-18, 2003

Chairpersons
Lucia Berman-Rossi, Jennifer Davis and Holly Fischer-Engel

The Boston Planning Committee

Frank Bartolmeo	Bonnie Engelhardt	Susan Lalone
Karen Buetens	Beth Fraster	Mary Lisbon
Marcia Cohen	Diane Haslett	Sandra Lyons
Jennifer Donnellan	Paul Hodlin	Meg MacPherson
Trudy Duffy	Catherine Horkan	Jennifer Wittlin

Executive Committee
of the International Board of Directors of AASWG, Inc., 2003

Toby Berman-Rossi, President
Barry University School of Social Work, Miami Shores, FL

Nancy E. Sullivan, Vice President
Memorial University of Newfoundland,
School of Social Work, St. John's, NL

Robert Salmon, Treasurer,
Hunter College School of Social Work, New York, NY

Timothy B. Kelly, Secretary,
Chair, Symposia Site Planning Committee, Webmaster,
Glasgow Caledonian University, Glasgow, Scotland

Raymie H. Wayne, General Secretary,
West Simsbury, CT

John H. Ramey, Past General Secretary, Editor, *Social Work with Groups Newsletter* and Chapter Representative, Northeast Ohio, University of Akron, Akron, OH

Michael W. Wagner, Chapter Representative, New York Red Apple, Chair, Chapter Development
The Children's Aid Society, New York, NY

Carolyn Knight, Ex-officio, Co-chair, Commission on Group Work in Social Work Education, Chair, Endowment Committee
School of Social Work, University of Maryland
Baltimore County, Baltimore, MD

We would also like to acknowledge the sponsorship of Boston University and the support of Dean Wilma Peebles. Professor Trudy Duffy led the B.U. efforts and helped make the Symposium a success. We would also like to acknowledge the support of two Boston agencies – The Big Sister Association *of Greater Boston* and The Planned Parenthood League of Massachusetts. Both agencies supported the symposium and subsequent proceedings in many important ways, reinforcing their strong belief in and understanding of the importance of group work as a modality of treatment.

We want to express our sincere gratitude to the Symposium Planning Committee, named above, who put in long hours and devoted much of their personal time to the 2003 Symposium. We talked, debated, argued and fought for our ideas, and in turn, made sure the symposium offered challenging workshops, innovative papers and a warm, welcoming atmosphere where attendees could relax, have fun, learn, and enjoy the company of fellow group workers. We also thank the Massachusetts Chapter of the Association for the Advancement of Social Work with Groups, Inc. We greatly admire everyone's dedication and hard work.

It is also important that we specifically acknowledge the support of several very special people, starting with Toby Berman-Rossi, who was the former President of the International Board of AASWG and Professor at Barry University. While she was the mother of one of the Symposium Co-Chairs and Editors of the Proceedings, she mothered us all by making sure we were nurtured and cared for throughout the sometimes grueling process of planning a Symposium! We also thank Tim Kelly, who provided us with invaluable information and support from both Florida and Scotland, and John Ramey, whose attention to detail made our symposium materials professional and accessible. We send a heartfelt thank you to Jennifer Davis, one of our Symposium Co-Chairs, for putting in countless hours and making the symposium possible. Finally, a thank you to our partners who encouraged us to work when we didn't have the energy and gave us moral support to do something we never thought we could. Chad Engel, Andrew Motta and David Wagner, thank you.

Dedication

The 2003 AASWG International Symposium and the subsequent Proceedings would not have been possible without the help, guidance and support of Toby Berman-Rossi, to whom these Proceedings are dedicated. Toby was a generous and devoted woman who spent much of her lifetime teaching and promoting group work. She was respected and admired by many, including her students, colleagues and fellow group workers. Toby exhibited a great deal of both strength *and* warmth, which made us all want to be near her, learn from her and make her proud. During the years we planned the International Symposium, Toby was the President of the International Board of AASWG. She is also the mother of one of the Symposium Co-Chairs, Lucia Berman-Rossi.

As Symposium Co-Chairs, it was always clear to us that Toby was there for us. She welcomed phone calls at any time of day or night and was quick to answer questions and give suggestions. When in Boston, she made a point to take us out to dinner to "feed our souls" and let us know how much she appreciated our efforts. She had a way of making us feel like we were being nurtured and taken care of as she pushed us to be the best we could be. Toby made us all want to be better group workers, better social workers and educators, and better human beings, and, through her teaching and her personal example, she taught us how to accomplish those goals.

This book is dedicated to the memory of Toby Berman-Rossi, our personal and professional mentor. You are one of the smartest and strongest women we've ever known, and we will never forget you. We love you and miss you.

About the editors

Lucia Berman-Rossi, LICSW, manages a small private practice providing clinical supervision and consultation services for various agencies. Her past experiences have included working in reproductive health at Planned Parenthood in Massachusetts, beginning SafeLink, the first statewide domestic violence hotline in Massachusetts and hospital and school social work. In addition to her practice, she is balancing board commitments with raising her daughter, Olive and is on the board of directors of the Massachusetts Alliance on Teen Pregnancy. She has served on both the local Massachusetts and international AASWG boards.

Marcia B. Cohen, LCSW, Ph.D. is Professor at the University of New England School of Social Work, where she has been on the faculty since 1988. She teaches courses in social group work, multi-level practice and social welfare policy. She provides consultation to and serves on the board of several local agencies. Marcia has been a member of AASWG since 1991 and has served two terms on the AASWG Board of Directors. She shares in the raising of Marx, a Bernese Mountain Dog.

Holly Fischer-Engel, LICSW, is the former Director of Group Mentoring at the Big Sister Association *of Greater Boston,* where she ran groups for girls in schools and community centers throughout the Greater Boston area and supervised group work staff and MSW interns. Her clinical experience also includes working in residential treatment centers for boys in DSS and DYS custody, as well as an outpatient addictions unit at a local Boston hospital. Holly has served on both the local and international AASWG Board of Directors, and is the former President of the local chapter. Holly currently has a full time job at home caring for her three young children - Sophia, Lucas and Evan.

The contributors

Janice Andrews-Schenk, MSW, Ph.D. (1944-2005) Jan received her MSW from Washington University and her PhD from the University of Maryland. She was very active in the Association for the Advancement of Social Work with Groups (AASWG) and served as its Vice-President from 2003-2005. Jan was the author of dozens of articles and two books, *The Road Not Taken* (with Michael Reisch) and *Rebellious Spirit: Gisela Konopka*. She was a Professor of Social Work at the University of St. Thomas in St. Paul, Minnesota, where she was held in high esteem by colleagues and students. Janice died while these Proceedings were being compiled.

Michael G. Chovanec, Ph.D., LICSW, LMFT. Michael is a tenured Assistant Professor at the College of St. Catherine/University of St. Thomas School of Social Work in St. Paul, Minnesota and has taught for the past ten years in the areas of Social Work Methods and Human Behavior and the Social Environment. He has been a clinician for the past 28 years and currently works part-time as coordinator and group facilitator for a county domestic abuse program for men who batter that he helped develop in 1988. Michael's group work experience includes a domestic abuse group, parenting groups, a day treatment group for adults with major mental illness and an educational/support group for families who have experienced mental illness. Michael is a licensed Clinical Social Worker, and Marriage and Family Therapist in the state of Minnesota. Michael can be reached at mgchovanec@stkate.edu.

Dianne Cullen. Dianne has been responsible for coordination and delivery of youth programs in the non-profit sector since 1999. She is currently a Youth Outreach Worker, responsible for youth program development & delivery in Haliburton County. Her background includes extensive experience in Health Care (RN), Social Service and the Justice field. She has received awards of recognition for her work in the design and delivery of intervention programs for children, and youth violence prevention and life skills programs. Her affiliations include AASWG; Canadian Bar - ADR Section; and The Network (for conflict resolution). Dianne can be reached at dvcullen@rogers.com.

Arielle Dylan, MSW, RSW. Arielle is currently a doctoral candidate at the Faculty of Social Work at the University of Toronto. She is affiliated with the AASWG and the Ontario College of Social Workers and Social Service Workers.

Mari Ann Graham, Ph.D., MSW. Mari Ann received her Ph. D. from Case Western Reserve University and her MSW from the University of Nebraska at Omaha. She currently directs the MSW Program and is Associate Professor at the College of St. Catherine/University of St. Thomas School of Social Work in St. Paul, Minnesota, where she also teaches practice courses, supervises clinical research projects and directs the Spirituality Institute. Mari Ann can be reached at magraham@stthomas.edu.

Juli Kempner, Esq., L.M.S.W., R.Y.T. Juli is a member of the Association of the Bar of the City of New York, the National Association of Social Workers, and the Association for the Advancement of Social Work with Groups. Juli is currently the Executive Director of the Georgia Law Center for the Homeless, a not for profit agency in Atlanta, Georgia, which provides free legal services for homeless people. Juli can be reached at julimsw@hotmail.com.

Carol Kuechler, M.S.W., Ph.D., L.I.S.W. Carol is Associate Professor at the School of Social Work, College of St. Catherine/University of St. Thomas, St. Paul, MN. She teaches research, clinical supervision and program management, and social group work in the graduate program. Carol provides supervision for licensure, is a faculty in the school's Supervision Institute, and conducts research projects related to supervision for individuals and groups. Carol can be reached at cfkuechler@stkate.edu.

Paule McNicoll, MSW, Ph.D. Paule is Associate Professor at the University of British Columbia School of Social Work and Family Studies. She teaches graduate and undergraduate group work courses and does research on the intersections between group work, social justice, culture, health and mental health. Paule can be reached by email at paule.mcnicoll@ubc.ca.

Lynne Mitchell, M.E.S., M.Ed., R.S.W. Lynne is a Registered Social Worker in private practice in Toronto, Canada, with a special interest in youth and families. She is also a member of the Ontario Association of Consultants, Counsellors, Psychometrists and Psychotherapists. She conducts workplace Parenting Support Groups, workshops, and training in group facilitation. She is one of the editors of "Social Work With Groups: Social Justice Through Personal, Community and Societal Change" and sits on the executive of the Toronto chapter of the AASWG. She recently completed a three-year term as a Board member of the AASWG. Lynne can be reached at lynnemitchell@sympatico.ca.

Paule McNicoll, MSW, Ph.D. Paule is Associate Professor at the University of British Columbia School of Social Work and Family Studies. She teaches graduate and undergraduate group work courses and does research on the intersections between group work, social justice, culture, health and mental health. Paule can be reached by email at paule.mcnicoll@ubc.ca.

David Prichard, Ph.D. Dave is Professor of Social Work at the University of New England. He maintains a private practice specializing in trauma and consults widely with health care professionals in developing secondary trauma debriefing protocol. He has written and presented throughout Europe and the United States on issues related to trauma, specifically the reconceptualization of trauma to include individuals secondarily impacted by traumatic events. David may be reached at dprichard@une.edu.

Jenny Schwartz, LGSW. Jenny is the Community Development Associate at the Minneapolis Jewish Federation. She has an MSW from the School of Social Work, College of St. Catherine/University of St. Thomas in St. Paul, MN and a BA in Communication Arts and Women's Studies from the University of Wisconsin-Madison. Jenny can be reached at jenniferschwartz@hotmail.com.

E. Michelle Sullivan, Ph.D., RSW. Michelle is an Assistant Professor in the School of Social Work at Memorial University of Newfoundland and Labrador. Her teaching responsibilities cover research and program evaluation, clinical skills and social work theory at both the undergraduate and graduate levels. Her funded research agenda includes the area of community capacity building and youth engagement in social policy development. Michelle is also an active member of a thriving private practice group focusing on child and family mental health issues. Michelle can be reached at Sullivan@mun.ca.

Nancy E. Sullivan, Ph.D., R.S.W. Nancy is a faculty member at the School of Social Work at Memorial University of Newfoundland, Canada, where she coordinates the MSW and PhD programs. She is a longtime groupwork practitioner, educator, and author, and was President of the Association for the Advancement of Social Work with Groups at the time the 25th Symposium was held. Nancy can be reached at nancys@mun.ca.

Introduction

Marcia B. Cohen

We are all drawn to work with groups for various reasons. Maybe you were in a group that helped you, maybe you kept hearing the fun group workers were having down the hall in the other classroom, or maybe you believe people are great at helping each other. Group workers know that feeling they have in a group where it all feels like it 'works'. We know the power that comes from 'strengths in numbers' and 'all in the same boat phenomena (Gitterman, 1979, p. 15, as cited in Lee, J. & Swenson, C. 2005).' We know well the magic of social work with groups.

Our theme for the 25th Annual International Group Work Symposium, 'Creating Connections: Celebrating the Power of Groups', was aimed at highlighting the effectiveness and power of groups, including groups both in the field and groups in the classroom. In planning for the symposium, we all felt an excitement about the idea of power in group work and were eager to work together to make this a powerful symposium. We had a wealth of abstracts to read, evaluate and choose from. As a result, many excellent papers and workshops were presented during the three days of the symposium, which marked our quarter century anniversary. The symposium itself represented a wealth of opportunities to create connections across geographical regions and boundaries. The papers in this Proceedings reflect the many presentations which made this 25th Annual International Group Work Symposium a success. They reflect the power of groups in a wide range of settings and with a variety of populations.

Mark Chovanec's paper, 'Innovations in Group Work with Abusive Men: Theories that Promote Engagement and Empowerment,' presents an important and innovative strengths oriented approach to working with abusive men utilizing reactive theory, the stages of change model and motivational interviewing. He demonstrates the increase in engagement and empowerment which are the benefits of this group work approach. The short-term goal of this model is to increase men's engagement in group treatment and reduce attrition. The long term goal, as with all treatment approaches for abusive men, is that of ending physical and emotional abuse. The hope discussed here is that these alternative approaches will provide a more respectful and human way of achieving these goals.

In another innovative paper, 'I Have a Dream': A Visioning Group for Adolescent First Nations Girls,' Arielle Dylan describes the 'I Have a Dream' project. This project utilizes a group model designed to empower pre-adolescent and adolescent girls, by helping them maintain their authentic selves in a 'girl poisoning' culture where mass communication peddles harmful values and superficial, unattainable standards. The girls who participated in this project, First Nation girls in the province of Ontario, struggle with the same sexist cultural context that all adolescent girls endure but also with the marginalization and racism that mainstream media and Western cultural values perpetuate. The 'I Have a Dream' model is a strengths-based, empowerment-focused, support-group model developed by Dylan to help girls ages 11 to 14 navigate the dangerous currents of adolescence and hold onto an intact, authentic self. This model produced positive results for group participants, including the opportunity to be masters of their own destiny within the group context. Group participation in itself was greatly empowering as group members felt personal efficacy in experiencing the outcome of their choices. The mutuality and peer support in the 'I Have a Dream' group enabled the girls to begin to understand and combat the oppressive forces of misogynistic dominant culture messages.

Mari Ann Graham's creative paper brings us into the social work classroom where she developed an innovative teaching strategy utilizing in-class book groups to simultaneously teach group work principles and diversity through the use of literature. As she describes it, literature can be used to teach the realities of diversity in contrast to text books which merely talk intellectually about diversity. In this model, students have a 'real life' group experience of mutual aid while meeting in small in-class groups to discuss a book and prepare a class presentation. The books were carefully chosen by the author and represent compelling novels which bring students into the worlds of members of marginalized groups. Graham provides a series of helpful suggestions to other educators interested in using literature groups to teach diversity.

Juli Kempner's thoughtful discussion of 'The Use of 'Twelve-Step' Concepts of Recovery in Group Work with Mentally Retarded and Developmentally Disabled Adults' provides insight into the question of whether cognitively impaired adults with substance misuse problems can benefit from a traditional 12-Step Recovery model. Using the literature and empirical research, Kempner demonstrates strong evidence of the beneficial effects of 12-Step Recovery groups for adults diagnosed with mental retardation and developmental disabilities. She concludes that the healing that comes from participation in 12-Step Groups is just as available and accessible to mentally retarded and developmentally disabled adults as it is to other populations because it is rooted in mutual aid which comes about through a group experience of learning and sharing hope, strength and experiences of recovery.

Carol Kuechler and Jennifer Schwartz's thought provoking paper 'Group Supervision: Motivation for Social Action' discusses the power inherent in the social action potential of group supervision. They present the findings from their focus group research which revealed the existence of social change components in group supervision which they categorized as supervisor-focused, group-focused and worker-focused. Their study demonstrates a strong connection between group supervision and social action, grounded in the interrelated roots of social group work and social work supervision. The authors suggest that supervisors should be prepared in attitude, knowledge and skill to guide their supervisees in the social action outcomes of group supervision.

Paule McNicholl's innovative breast cancer support group project, Dragon Boat racing is beautifully described in her paper, 'As if by Magic': Women with Breast Cancer, Dragon Boats and Healing in a Group.' Based on adventure therapy, a group of 'Dragon Boat' paddlers, all survivors of breast cancer, experienced strong mutual aid and physical well being through working together in dragon boat competitions. McNicoll analyses nine themes which emerged from focus group and questionnaire data obtained from group participants. She looks at metaphors used to describe the group experience in order to capture the magic of the Dragon Boat project's outcomes. As McNicoll observes, some life situations are so painful that accessing them directly is overwhelming. Metaphors offer an alternative pathway to explore and heal from these experiences.

Lynn Mitchell and Dianne Cullen's 'SAVE' Students Against Violence at Emery A Whole School Initiative; A Small Group Approach' presents an innovative collaborative effort of community agencies, the Toronto School District, and the Emery Collegiate Institute to address incidents of youth violence in a secondary school. This program is unique in that it was driven by student-defined goals and agendas. It provided an opportunity for students to meet during the school day with two skilled group facilitators and a group of their peers to discuss not just violence but also other challenges they experience daily. The group process, directed by the guidelines that the group participants developed themselves, allowed the youth opportunities to experience a different form of peer interaction, one that was respectful and supportive, while allowing them to be cognizant of their similarities and differences. The evaluation of this initiative indicated that the small group program model was effective in reaching students and building resources within the community in the area of youth violence prevention. The authors conclude that students participants in the program modified the school culture to one where they were less likely to engage in violent activities and more likely to experience an overall reduction of the impact of violence in their lives.

David Prichard's paper 'Group Work with Refugee Children in a Multicultural Bereavement Program' provides important content about work with traumatized refugee children in a bereavement group, examines the secondary impact of trauma work on group participants (members and facilitators) and explores implications for group workers working with traumatized populations. The model described is a multicultural program in a group-focused agency setting offering bereavement services. This program emphasizes pre-group and post-group debriefing sessions for facilitators who are, for the most part, untrained volunteers who receive bereavement group training though the agency. Examples of group process and content convey to the reader some of the horrors that this group addresses, Prichard discusses the potential traumatizing effect on group participants who witnesses the harrowing narratives of the most traumatized children in the group. The group is organized so that a refugee child struggling with the recent death of a family member from natural causes is in the same group as a refugee child who witnessed parental torture and murder in his country of origin. The author cautions multicultural programs to more carefully consider group composition and develop mechanisms to protect less traumatized group members. He also raises concerns about the potential impact of exposure to traumatic events on group facilitators as it has been found that such exposure may cause group workers to experience traumatic stress symptoms. Prichard calls on bereavement programs to integrate content on secondary trauma into their staff and volunteer training programs.

In a third paper focused on group work with youth, Nancy Sullivan and Michelle Sullivan provide insights into the opportunities and challenges of working with natural groups in their discussion of 'Creating Connections among Disadvantaged Youth: Toward Participation in Policy Development and Social Change.' They describe a project designed to enhance participation by excluded youth in a pre-formed group of participants in a program for youth living in poverty. The purpose of the project was to enhance participation by youth in social policy development through a community empowerment model based on principles of participatory democracy. The specific objectives included assisting excluded youth in identifying policy issues that impact on their lives by enhancing their skills and capacity to expand their understanding about social policy, to explore policy alternatives and policy development work, to gain experience in applying their skills as policy contributors and to increase knowledge regarding the process by which engagement in policy development happens. Youth participated in workshops which incorporated several activities which encouraged them to examine social policies relevant to their daily lives and enhanced their abilities to do so. The authors discuss the implications of this innovative project in increasing our awareness of the positive group process and useful outcomes that can be associated with working with natural groups.

These proceedings begin with a keynote address by the late Janice Andrews-Schenk which serves to ground all that follows in the historical and philosophical context of group work. In 'Common Elements in Philosophy and Method: A Brief History of Social Group Work in the United States,' Andrews traces the history of social group work in the US with an emphasis on its progressive and democratic philosophical underpinnings. Tracing the developments in our field from group work's early days in settlement houses, neighborhood centers, Y's, Jewish community centers, camps, scouts and labor unions through the merger with NASW in 1955, the founding of AASWG and the birth of the journal, *Social Work With Groups* in 1978, and culminating in our 25th Anniversary Symposium in Boston, Andrews describes a vibrant history in which the zeal of the early days of social group work has sustained itself through to the present. As we continue to mourn Jan's early death which occurred while these proceedings were being compiled, we recognize her ongoing contribution to social group work, which will continue to outlive her.

Reference

Lee, J. & Swenson, C. (2005). Mutual Aid: A Buffer Against Risk. In A. Gitterman and L. Shulman, (Eds.). *Mutual Aid Groups, Vulnerable and Resilient Populations, and the Life Cycle* (3rd ed.), New York: Columbia University Press.

1

Common elements in philosophy and method:

A brief history of social group work in the United States

Janice Andrews-Schenk

While groups have always been present in one form or another in the United States, organized social group work emerged out of a number of shifts in society in the late nineteenth and early twentieth centuries. These changes included industrialization, large population shifts from rural to urban centers and the enormous wave of immigration, mainly to U.S. urban areas. Group work as a field of practice during these turbulent times offered a philosophy that challenged the older, more established social service networks that generally 'distinguished sharply between the giver and the receiver' (Konopka, 1963, p. 3). Group work occurred in helping organizations that focused on mutual self-help, recreation and informal education; group work was practiced in settlements, neighborhood centers, Y's, Jewish centers, camps, scouts, labor union organizations and labor workers' schools.

In the 1920s, group work education found a home in schools of social work which began offering group work courses and eventually specializations in social group work. Group workers were actively engaged in interracial and multi-ethnic groups reflecting the importance of cultural issues in a pluralistic society. A progressive philosophy provided direction to social group work during its formative years. The fundamental philosophy related to the 'sanctity of the individual human being in an interdependent society' (Kaiser, 1948, p. 421). As Clara Kaiser pointed out early in its history, group work 'is rooted in our American culture in its religious, social, economic, and political aspects' (p.421).

Both in theory and in practice, social group work embraced a democratic way of life, social responsibility and an understanding of the human need to interact with others as an equal member. There was a 'recognition that the specific role of the group worker [was] to safeguard the potential of the individual within the group, while at the same time strengthening the group-as-a-whole' (Konopka, 1981, p. 111). To Gisela Konopka, the idea was as if social work had 'discovered gold' (p. 111) – it was that important.

Like all philosophies and practices, there have always been ideological differences in both theory and practice. The literature, from early on, argued about what the criteria should be for an experience to be called social group work or social work with groups. As early as the 1940s, group workers voiced a plea that group work be open to diversity in 'ideas and philosophy' (Kaiser, 1948, p. 427). Concepts derived from a number of thinkers in a variety of disciplines, including Simmel and Weber in sociology and Dewey and Follett in informal and progressive education, were balanced with Freud's psychoanalytic theory and Homan's systems theory. A healthy tension regarding what to emphasize brought forth a number of group work theoretical positions held together by the belief that the small group could provide members with the opportunity 'to shape their wants and desires and to affect the larger social structure,' (Abels and Abels, 1981, p. 147). As Sonia and Paul Abels declared, 'Group work's pedestal was hope' (p. 147).

After the National Conference on Social Work (NCSW) formed a group work section in 1935, group work became more closely associated with social work. In 1936, approximately fifty group workers met to form the National Association for the Study of Group Work under the leadership of Arthur Swift. When Louis Kraft, then Executive Director of the National Jewish Welfare Board, sat down in 1947 with an editor of *The Group* to reminisce about group work, he spoke directly to the passion of early group workers and their movement. 'We were a group of zealots', he said. These passionate group workers had a sense of mission and, as Kraft indicated, a belief in 'common elements in philosophy and method' (Reminiscing with Louis Kraft, 1947, pp.12-13).

By 1946, the organizational name was the American Association of Group Workers (AAGW) with membership of almost 2000 group workers (NASW records, AAGW section description, SWHA, 21) representing recreation, informal education, social work and group dynamics. That same year Grace Coyle (in Trecker, 1955, 340) presented a paper at NCSW announcing that group work 'as a method falls within social work as a method...' The audience agreed and leading group workers including Coyle and Trecker as well as Sanford Solander and others, actively worked toward the formation of the National Association of Social Workers (NASW). Between 1948 and 1949, several important group work books were published, including: Coyles' *Group Work with American Youth* 1948, Wilson and Ryland's *Social Group Work Practice* (1949), often referred to as the 'Green Bible,' and Konopka's *Therapeutic Group Work with Children (1949).* These three books covered the wide range of work in groups from more social groups to groups for those with emotional problems. All described group work as a method of intervention.

NASW was born in 1955 with five practice sections, including a group work section. AAGW membership was almost 3000 members representing 44 chapters in major cities, a small minority of the larger social work membership of around 22,000. While the majority of group workers supported the merger into NASW at the time, many spoke then and later of the losses this decision brought to group work. Pernell (1986, p.13) saw group work, as a method of social work, moving closer to a problem oriented philosophy and problem oriented agencies and away from leisure time activities and more recreational agencies. Others saw it as 'the death knell of group work as a unique methodology' (Glasser and Mayadas, 1986, p. 4). Ruth Middleman declared that the merger resulted in a number of losses that were 'largely not remembered or discussed' (1981, pp. 187-205). These included the move from the focus on the group to meet common problems and needs, from activities in favor of talk, from study and research on group process and from moving beyond members' interests.

With the end of AAGW also came the end of the association's quarterly journal, *The Group*. In its memory, Harleigh Trecker in 1995 edited a volume of selected articles that had appeared in *The Group* from 1939 to 1954 called *Group Work: Foundations and Frontiers* (1955). This volume included articles on the roots of democratic culture by Eduard Lindeman, definition of the function of the group worker by Grace Coyle, the effect of cultural variables on group work practice by Alan Klein, the place of agency structure, philosophy and policy in supporting group programs of social action by Helen Northern, resistance and hostility by Gisela Konopka, group work education in the last decade by Clara Kaiser – just to name a few.

After the NASW Delegate Assembly voted in 1962 to disband all the sections, including group work, critics of the merger grew. For many group workers, this period represented the biggest crisis in the history of group work (Andrews, 2001). Abels and Abels (1981) referred to the following years when schools of social work increasingly dropped group work specializations, and eventually even individual group work courses as the 'generocide' of group work.

Yet, group workers continued to actively theory-build and write. Catherine Papell and Beulah Rothman, in 1966, conceptualized three models: social goals, reciprocal and remedial, providing a clearer understanding of social group work. The Group Work Department at Boston University published the results of their work in 1965 that included a model for stages of group development (Garland, Jones and Kolodney). During the 1960s and 1970s, group workers such as William Schwartz, Helen Northen, Ruth Middleman, Gisela Konopka, Helen Phillips, Hans Falck, Alan Klein, Robert Vinter and others wrote important group workbooks. Some group workers, including Helen Northen, Alex Gitterman and Lawrence Shulman, also published books on the generic base of social work practice.

Not until 1978 and the publication of a new journal *Social Work with Groups: A Journal of Community and Clinical Practice*, under the editorship of Catherine Papell and Beulah Rothman, did group work articles again find a home. At the next annual meeting of the Council on Social Work Education, a key group of people – Katie Papell, Beulah Rothman and Ruth Middleman, who pulled in Paul and Sonia Abels, John Ramey, Ruby Pernell and others – called an informal meeting to plan a group work symposium. Middleman (1992, p. 28) later described the meeting: 'It was a dinner hour in a small room on an upper floor. About sixty people piled in, sitting on the floor and planning for a kick-off symposium ... the rest is history.' The same passion and 'missionary spirit' that motivated group workers in the 1930s to create a group work identity accompanied this rebirth of social group work.

The First Annual Group Work Symposium of what would become the Association for the Advancement of Social Work with Groups (AASWG) was held in 1979. The wildly successful conference, held in Cleveland to honor the work of Grace Coyle, 'felt like a group work party' to Katie Papell who remembers the 'excitement and thrill which consumed the [more than 350] social group workers' at the conference (Papell, 1997, p. 10).

The passion and zeal has continued. Group work has survived. Its resiliency is a testament to the persistence of a core of people as well as the strength of the method (Ramey, 1998). Group work ideology has stood up well over time because it is rooted in a clear understanding of the realities of human lives and the human condition. As Paul Ephross

(1998) has said, 'We were right then, we're right now.'

We gather this evening to celebrate the twenty-fifth anniversary of AASWG and the strength of social group work around the globe. The passion, zeal and spirit of a movement of people drawn together by common elements in philosophy and methods will determine its future.

References

Abels, P. and S. Abels. (1981). Social work's contextual purposes. In P. Abels and S. Abels (Eds.) *Social work with groups: Proceedings, 1979 Symposium*, (pp. 146-160). Louisville, KY: AASWG

Abels, P. and S. Abels. (1981). *Social work with groups: Proceedings, 1979 Symposium.* Louisville, KY: AASWG

Andrews, J. (2001, December). Group work's place in social work: A historical analysis. *Journal of Sociology and Social Welfare XXVIII*, 45-65

Coyle, G. (1948). *Group work and American youth.* New York: Harper and Row

Garland, J., Jones, H., and Kolodny, R., A model for stages of development in social work groups. In S. Bernstein (Ed.) *Exploration in group work: essays in theory and practice.* Boston: Boston University School of Social Work

Glasser, P. and Mayadas, N. (1986). The changing nature of social group work practice. In P. Glasser and N. Mayadas (Eds.). *Group workers at work: Theory and practice in the 80s.* (pp. 3-10). Totowa, NJ: Rowman and Littlefield

Kaiser, C. (1948). Current frontiers in social group work. *Proceedings of the National Conference of Social Work*, 418-428.

Konopka, G. (1963). *Social group work: A helping process.* Englewood Cliffs, NJ: Prentice-Hall

Konopka, G. (1981). Perspective on social group work. In S. Abels and P. Abels (Eds.). *Social Work with Groups: Proceedings, 1979 Symposium* (pp. 111-116). Louisville, KY: AASWG

Middleman, R. (1981). The use of programs. In S. Abels and P. Abels. (Eds.). *Social work with groups: Proceedings, 1979 Symposium.* (pp. 187-205). Louisville: KY: Committee for the Advancement of Social Work with Groups.

Middleman, R. (1992). Group work and the Heimlich maneuver; Unchoking social work education. In E. Fike and B. Rittner (Eds.) *Working from strengths: The essence of group work.* (pp. 16-39). Miami Shores, FL: Center for Group Work Studies

NASW Records, *AAGW section description.* (p. 21). Minneapolis, MN: University of Minnesota Social Welfare History Archives

Northen, H. Historical trends. (1994, May). In M. Campbell (Ed.), *Tulane studies in social welfare (XIX): Social group work in the 1990s,* (pp.13-38). New Orleans: Tulane University

Papell, C. and Rothman, B.. (1966). Social work models: Possession and heritage. *Journal of Education for Social Work 2(2),* 66-77

Papell, C. (1997). Thinking about thinking about group work: Thirty years later. *Social work with groups 20(4),* 5-17

Ramey, J. (1998). Interview with the author

Reminiscing with Louis Kraft. (1947, October). *The Group 10(1),* 12-13

Trecker, H. (Ed.). (1955). *Group work: Foundations and frontiers.* Hebron, CT: Practitioners' Press, Inc

Wilson, G. and Ryland, G. (1949*). Social group work practice: The creative use of the social process.* Hebron, CT: Practitioner's Press

2

Innovations in groupwork with abusive men:

Theories that promote engagement and empowerment

Michael George Chovanec

Domestic abuse is a social problem that impacts women, their families and the community. Bachman (1994), from a national victimization survey estimated two to four million American women are beaten every year. In 1996, 30% of all female murder victims were slain by their husband or boyfriends (Federal Bureau of Investigation, 1997). Partner abuse also greatly impacts children. Davidson (1994) reports that between 3.3 and 10 million children witness violence in their homes. In 50 to 70% of cases in which a parent abuses another parent, the children are also physically abused (Bowker et al., 1988). In addition to the emotional cost of being a victim, perpetrator or witness of abuse, economic costs are staggering. Miller et al. (1996), in review of a data from the National Institute of Justice, found that domestic violence costs 67 billion dollars per year in property damage, medical costs, mental health care, police and fire services, victim services and lost worker productivity.

The groupwork response to the domestic abuse problem

To address this significant social problem group work has traditionally been the treatment of choice (Healy, Smith & O'Sullivan, 1998; Pirog-

Good & Stets, 1985) and is recommended by the majority of state standards (Austin & Dankwort, 1999). By the mid-1980s approximately 195 programs were developed (Pirog-Good & Stets-Kealey, 1985). The involuntary nature of court-ordered treatment is frequently seen in the domestic abuse field. Roberts (1982), in his national survey, reported that 66% of programs surveyed received 40% to 95% of referrals from the court system. Gondolf (1985), in a qualitative study of 50 men who had completed domestic abuse treatment, reported that 90% of the men reported requesting help only after their partner had left or had threatened to leave. Thus, even if the potential client is not court-ordered, forces both internal and external impact their decision about whether to accept treatment or not.

Group programs range from process oriented (Jennings, 1987, 1990; Caplan & Thomas, 1995, 1999) to the more structured approach, integrating cognitive behavioral, social learning, communication and feminist theories (Edleson & Tolman, 1992). The Duluth model based on the educational program developed in Duluth Minnesota (Pence & Paymar, 1993) is probably the most widely applied domestic abuse program. The model defines abuse broadly to include emotional and economic abuse, and the use of intimidation, coercion and/or threats. The basic assumption is that men abuse women primarily to maintain power and control over women. The facilitator role includes holding men accountable for their abuse, keeping the group discussion on issues of violence, abuse and control, and challenging, not colluding, with men's abusive belief system. In addition, facilitators are to support reflective and critical thinking and provide new information on alternatives to controlling behavior in relationships (Pence & Paymar, 1993).

Other domestic abuse models have advocated for greater emphasis on process rather than structure while retaining the major treatment goals of reducing physical and emotional abuse and helping men take responsibility for their abusive behavior (Jennings, 1987; Thomas & Caplan, 1999). Jennings (1987) advocates for an unstructured, closely supervised self-help group program that focuses on the client's agenda for change and provides problem-solving and interpersonal skills. He argues that this format provides an opportunity for greater use of mutual peer support and enhances empathy skills. He also suggests that traditional programs place too high of an expectation on both the abuser and group facilitator for change in behavior and attitudes toward women in a short amount of time (Jennings, 1990). His model emphasizes relapse prevention and building supports that maintain changes made by men in the program.

Thomas and Caplan (1999) propose a model developed through work with abusive men and training facilitators at the McGill Domestic Abuse Clinic. They identify 56 useful group techniques that focus on group process, enhancing participation of involuntary clients within groups. Group techniques are categorized into process, inclusion and linking interventions. The group facilitator uses process interventions to identify the emotional message behind the client's statement and reflects the client's world-view. Major emotional themes found in domestic abuse clients' stories include betrayal, abandonment, and powerlessness. Linking interventions are used to connect individual issues with others in the group and allow the group leader to make generalized statements about the group itself. Inclusion interventions encourage uninvolved group members to join the group discussion and include didactic and projective exercises that allow group members to voice their opinion without being singled out. The interventions of process, linking and inclusion have been further explored on how they can be used to help facilitators stay in the moment in uncomfortable exchanges with clients to further growth and avoid a confrontational impasse (Caplan & Thomas, 2002).

Groupwork effectiveness in domestic abuse treatment

Gondolf (1997b) identified five published reviews of approximately 30 single-site evaluations (Eisikovits & Edelson, 1989; Gondolf, 1991, 1997; Rosenfeld, 1992; Tolman &Bennett, 1990). He reported approximately 60% to 80% of program completers end their violent behavior with fewer reducing their threats and verbal abuse. Outcomes measures included reduction in the conflict tactics scale as completed by participants, their partners or both, post-treatment contact with police, and court records of post-treatment convictions, participants' self reports on attitudes toward women, jealousy, anger, assertiveness, hostility, coping methods and depression and self report of physical violence by participants, partners or both. A variety of methodological flaws have been identified in these evaluations including low response rates (30% to 45%), self-report measures, short-term follow-up (generally 6 months), lack of control groups and failure to account for intervening variables, i.e. accounting for program dropouts.

A limited number of studies with control groups found mixed results (Davis, Taylor & Maxwell, 1998; Feder & Forde, 2000; Palmer, Brown & Barrera, 1992). Control groups consisted of men referred to probation or community service instead of programming (Davis et al. 1998; Feder and Forde, 2000) or men not offered treatment (Palmer et al. 1992). The latter was the most controversial and probation was allowed to refer control group men to treatment if their partners were found at risk. Assessments were done at sentencing, 6 months and 12 months. Davis, et al. (1998) found significant fewer re-arrests for the 6-month program, but with no differences in victim reports of new abusive incidents between program and controls. Palmer et al. (1992) found significantly fewer re-arrests for the treatment group (10%) compared to the no treatment controls (31%). Feder and Forde (2000) found no differences between program and controls in men's' arrests, probation violations, attitudes or men and women reports of abuse.

The low numbers of women reports on partners' abusive behavior and lack of data on partners' relationships with men at follow-up weaken the above studies. Also dropouts in these experimental designs were considered part of the program, although they may have had either limited or no contact with the program. Typically the other key components of community intervention, i.e., court, probation and jail, need to respond to those men dropping out of treatment. Gondolf (2001) suggests the need to have broader evaluations that include the whole community intervention system of which the program is one component. In addition, a majority of re-assaults occur within the first 3 months of a program when men are being exposed to the program (Gondolf, 1997c, 2000). In the midst of the involuntary nature of the problem, and a host of other impacting factors, i.e., depression and alcoholism, it does not seem unusual that abusive behavior may continue as men become engaged in the treatment process.

Impact of attrition
on treatment effectiveness

Attrition is a major factor impacting the effectiveness of domestic abuse treatment. Daly and Pelowski (2000) in a review of 16 domestic abuse studies report attrition rates ranging from 22% to 99% depending on which point in the treatment process one evaluates from (Daly & Pelowski, 2000). Gondolf & Foster (1991), examining attrition from initial contact to treatment completion, reported only 10% of men completing the program. These percentages are significant given that in 1997 136,000 men were arrested for domestic violence and 86% were ordered into counseling (Hagen, 1998).

High rates of attrition, with dropouts left out of the outcome analysis, can seriously inflate treatment success. Most importantly, attrition threatens the safety of women. Women often remain with partners who enroll in domestic abuse programs expecting them to complete the program and no longer abuse them (Gondolf, 1988). However, dropouts are more likely to re-offend than program graduates putting their partners in dangerous potentially abusive situations (Gondolf, 1997c; Dutton, 1986; Edleson & Gruszunski, 1988; Palmer, Brown & Barrera, 1992; Shupe, Stacy & Hazelwood, 1987). In one study dropouts were two to three times more likely to re-offend shortly after intake (Gondolf, 1997c).

Attrition research suggests a variety of factors contribute to dropout including unemployment, being unmarried and fatherless, having lower incomes, and less education (Daly & Pelowski (2000). In addition, the relationship between court referral and dropout has been inconsistent across studies.

While many studies examining attrition in domestic abuse treatment have focused on demographic variables, violence related factors and client pathology, a limited number of studies have examined men's level of motivation or commitment to attend (Daly & Pelowski, 2000). DeMaris (1989) found that men, who highly rated the importance of stopping their violent behavior, were twice as likely to complete the program. Cadsky and associates (1996) found that those men with higher treatment congruence, who were willing to report abusing their partner in the intake, were more likely to complete the program.

Standard confrontational approaches impact attrition

Historically, due to safety concerns of the victims, batterer programs focused primarily on stopping physical abuse with little attention to the change process. A common goal of domestic abuse treatment is to help batterers accept responsibility for their abusive behavior and a confrontational approach has supported this. The Duluth model, a standard in the domestic abuse field, focuses on confronting men's rationalizations and challenges them to acknowledge responsibility for their abusive behavior (Pence & Paymar, 1993). While the goal of helping batterers accept responsibility for their abusive behavior is common, the means to accomplishing this goal is controversial.

While the effects of confrontation used in domestic abuse groups have not been researched, adverse effects can be found in other settings. Confrontational approaches were introduced in the chemical dependency field in the 1970s and 1980s (Thomas & Yoshioka, 1989). Research in chemical dependency treatment support the use of empathic rather than confrontational interventions for successful outcomes (Miller, 1985, Miller & Rollnick, 1991) Lambert and Bergin (1994) found that clients most at risk of deterioration within group treatment were those with low self-esteem and impaired self-concepts. High-risk clients fit the description of many batterers (Dutton & Starzomski, 1993; Hamberger & Hastings, 1991). Personality disorders and men with history of severe child abuse are common in this population (Hamberger & Hastings, 1989; Hamberger et al, 2000; DeHart, Kenneryly, Burke & Follingstad, 1999; Faulkner, Cogan, Nolder & Shooter, 1991).

The extent to which confrontational approaches contribute to the attrition problem in domestic abuse treatment is difficult to assess. Only two studies examined client motivation in regards to attrition suggesting a level of commitment to change (Cadsky et al., 1996) and congruence between client and treatment goals (DeMaris, 1989) are key for treatment completers. Using a confrontational approach without acknowledging client's readiness for change limits engaging men in the treatment process. If men drop out of treatment, the research suggests women are put at risk for future abuse (Gondolf, 1997; Dutton, 1986; Edleson & Gruszunski, 1988; Palmer, Brown & Barrera, 1992; Shupe, Stacy & Hazelwood, 1987). Murphy and Baxter (1997) raise the question to what extent does this confrontational approach support the goals of safety and justice for battered women?

The confrontational approach also calls into question what facilitators are modeling for abusive men when using a confrontational approach to change behavior. With increased resistance to confrontations the issues of power and control are more likely to be present between therapist and client. This mirrors the dynamics many men have grown up with who enter domestic abuse treatment and contradicts the effort in traditional programs like the Duluth model, to move men from inequality in power and control to more equality in relationships (Pence & Paymar, 1993).

Best practices in domestic abuse treatment

In recent years there has been a call for guidelines for empirically based treatment in clinical practice (Howard & Jenson, 1999; Howard, Edmond & Vaughn, 2005). In domestic abuse, guidelines for best practices are in demand as states develop standards for treatment (Austin & Dankwort, 1999). In the domestic abuse treatment literature there is no empirical evidence that distinguishes one modality over another (Tolman & Bennett, 1990, Saunders, 1996, Gondolf, 2000). However, variations in format appear to have some effect on treatment effectiveness. Groups offering more structure within a didactic format are more effective than didactic and discussion and self-help groups (Edleson & Syers, 1990, 1991; Gondolf, 1999). Also short and long term treatment produce similar reductions in assault (Edleson and Syers, 1989; Gondolf, 1999).

Given the high attrition rates found in the literature (Gondolf, 1997; Daly & Pelowski, 2000), best practices need to include ways to better engage men in the treatment process in addition to abuse reduction. Tolman and Bhosley (1987) and Brekke (1989) found orientating potential group members to programming reduced attrition. Stosny (1994), used video in a domestic abuse program, dramatizing spouse abuse from the perspective of a young boy, which significantly increased attendance and group participation. Both components need further research to confirm their use in terms of best practices. Neither are included in current state guidelines for domestic abuse treatment (Austin & Dankwort, 1999).

Innovations in group work with abusive men

A more systematic approach to examining the engagement process in domestic abuse treatment has been through the application of a variety of theories/practice models. These theories/practice models are just beginning to be applied to the domestic abuse field and deserve attention as potential best practices.

Reactance theory, originating from social psychology, examines motivational arousal and how one behaves when under perceived or actual coercion. The theory assumes that everyone has a set of behaviors, which they are free to exercise at any given point in time. If some of those behavioral freedoms valued by an individual are threatened or eliminated, one will experience 'reactance', a motivational drive to restore those freedoms (Brehm & Brehm, 1981). Applied to domestic abuse treatment, men court-ordered or pressured from others to attend, have lost the freedom to leave treatment without negative consequences. The theory suggests that men court-ordered or pressured into a program should demonstrate high levels of reactance or motivational arousal which is presented through an array of predictable behaviors, i.e., hostility toward group leader and passive participation. Chovanec (1995) confirms what the theory suggests by finding high levels of reactance in men entering a domestic abuse program. A variety of interventions have been suggested to either reduce or increase reactance with individuals (Rooney, 1992, Norcross, Beutler & Clarkin, 1998) and more recently with groups (Rooney & Chovanec, 2004). For example, reactance can be reduced by acknowledging pressures men experience upon entering treatment and providing choices in programming. Assessing reactance early in the treatment process has been found useful in engaging general practice clients early on in the treatment process and increases the chances for successful outcomes (Prochaska, Norcross & DiClemente, 1995; Beutler & Berren, 1995; Beutler, Kim, Davidson, Karno & Fisher, 1996; and Groth-Marnat, 1997). However little attention has been given in examining reactance in the domestic abuse setting.

The Stages of Change model is another promising framework for addressing the attrition problem through examining the process of change men go through as they enter domestic abuse treatment. The model evolved through research examining how people overcome addictive behaviors such as smoking, drinking and emotional stress (Prochaska, Norcross & DiClemente, 1995; Norcross, Beutler &

Clarkin, 1998). The model suggests people go through a series of five stages to change their addictive behavior. In the pre-contemplation stage, clients do not perceive themselves as having a problem others in their environment identify them having. In the contemplation stage, clients identify having a problem but are not yet ready to act on them. In the preparation stage, clients are ready to make preliminary steps towards change. Those preliminary steps toward change become more consistent in the action stage. Finally, clients maintain their changed behaviors in the maintenance stage.

The stages of change scale (SOCS) has been developed for assessing client change process (McConnaughy, DiClemente, Prochaska & Velicer, 1989). Application of this instrument has helped to build growing evidence that pre-contemplators are common among those clients seeking mental health treatment. Also pre-contemplators have been confirmed in samples of alcohol abuse (DiClemente & Hughes, 1990), cocaine abuse and juvenile delinquency (Prochaska et al, 1994).

Motivational interviewing is another useful framework evolving out of the chemical dependency literature that potentially can prove useful in better engaging abusive men in treatment. The framework developed in work with chemical dependency clients, including those who opposed entering treatment (Miller & Rollnick, 1991). Resistance is reframed as ambivalence and strategies are offered to address it. For example, clients are asked to identify both negative and positive consequences of changing their behavior. In addition, the client self-motivating statements towards change are identified and supported. For example, a client may discuss how he has tried to change in the past. If not elicited by the client, the worker initiates these statements through self-reflective questions asked the client.

While the framework was developed independently of the Stages of Change model, it has been used together and applied to work with domestic abuse clients (Murphy & Baxter, 1997; Daniels & Murphy, 1997). Daniels and Murphy (1997) point out that while most domestic abuse programs assume an unmotivated client who is coerced into treatment, the majority of interventions work best with men who have accepted they have a problem and want to work on it. For example in the Duluth model the facilitator role includes facilitating reflective and critical thinking, provide new information and teaches non-controlling relationship skills (Pence & Paymar, 1993). Daniels and Murphy (1997) suggest that most domestic abuse programs overlook the process men go through of weighing the pros and cons of changing their abusive behavior. They provide an array of interventions that more accurately pace with men as they move through the stages of change. They also validate the value of groups in which men at later stages of change can inform and challenge those men unwilling or ambivalent about changing their abusive behavior.

Specific application of innovations for domestic abuse treatment

Pre-group planning

Pre-group planning is important in developing a program that responds effectively to men initially resistant to treatment and that anticipates the varying degrees of readiness for change men present. Reactance theory suggests that increased choices and clarifying negotiable and non-negotiable rules reduce reactance (Brehm & Brehm, 1981). Thus it is important to identify in the program where choices can be offered and to clarify negotiable and non-negotiable elements of the program. For example, court referred men can be encouraged early in the intake process to check out other programs in regards to cost and time available before committing to one program. Men who are required to complete various tasks and exercises for completion of the program (i.e., control plan, empathy exercise) may be given choices in terms of when they complete them. Applying the stages of change model to domestic abuse treatment suggests that men will be at varying stages of change when entering the program. While a majority of men can be anticipated to be in the pre-contemplation stage (not see a problem), a number of men may not. O'Hare (1996) assessed client level of motivation for change and found that in a sample of court-ordered mental health clients 28% were already making efforts to change their behavior. The following figure from Rooney and Chovanec (2004), developed in applying reactance theory and stages of change to involuntary groups, is applicable to domestic abuse treatment programs. Many domestic abuse programs have a combination of mandated and non-mandated clients. Men enter domestic abuse treatment with a variety of pressures to change their abusive behavior, including a court order (mandated), which is more visible and pressures from partners, friends or professionals that are not. This suggests facilitators need to ask early on about the pressures to change their behavior that men enter treatment with.

Figure 1
Involuntary clients and groups: Change motivation

LEGAL STATUS	Low initial motivation for change	High initial motivation for change
Mandated	1 Anticipated type of client found in mandated groups	2 'Hidden' semi-voluntary clients found in mandated groups.
Non mandated	3 Ambivalent members in otherwise voluntary group i.e. constrained participation in a parenting group	4 Highly motivated clients usually found in voluntary groups.

Another important element of pre-group planning is the development of a prepared opening statement that is presented to men in either a first group or an orientation meeting with one or more men. This opening statement allows the facilitator to join with the potential group members by anticipating some of the major questions and concerns men bring with them as they enter the program. The statement can also be used to reduce reactance and support men's preliminary efforts towards change. The following is an example of an opening statement one could use for men entering a domestic abuse program:

Welcome to the program. I know many of you may feel you have been forced to come here. Many men who are in similar situations never make it to orientation. I support your choice in attending the program. (Validate choices made) You may be anticipating that we will try to force you to change. The reality is that no one can make you change. (Comment on change process) All we ask is that you listen to what we have to say and take the bits and pieces of the program that make sense to you and that can help you avoid future problems and/or contact with the court system. You may also be fearing you will be judged as guilty or worse shamed for the incident that brings you in. Many of you have already gone through the court system. We are not here to judge you as guilty or innocent for the charges you bring with you. Our focus is on helping you learn from whatever incident brings you in. Our task is to create a safe environment for men to examine their actions and learn from their mistakes. We will not tolerate physical or verbal abuse within group sessions. Those men who are abusive within the group will be asked to leave. In regards to confidentiality we ask that all men keep confidential what is said within group. We cannot force group members to do this but expect men will do this in respect for others within group. (Clarify non-negotiable group rules) The exception to confidentiality for me as the facilitator is that if you tell me that you are in danger of hurting yourself or others I need to by law, report that information to other professionals or the authorities.

Pre-group orientation with an opening statement like the one above provides an opportunity to engage men early in the process, to orientate them to the program and to assess where they are in the change process. Expectations of the program are clarified as well as negotiable elements or choices in the program. These sessions can also raise the opportunity for contracting around other more voluntary problems acknowledged by potential members such as improving relationships with their children.

Figure 2 opposite adopted from Rooney and Chovanec (2004) links interventions to group stages and to stages of change. It provides a useful guide as we continue the application of the innovations throughout the course of domestic abuse treatment.

Beginning stage

In anticipation of pre-contemplators focus is on exploring the change process of men entering treatment. Prochaska et al. (1994) suggest the change process has both an experiential and behavioral component. In the beginning of treatment, focus is on the experiential. This includes men thinking about or reacting emotionally to abusive behavior they have been accused of. Facilitators use reflective listening skills and encourage self-evaluation of the situation. The goal is to move men from not seeing a problem to considering they may have a problem and might want to address it. Negative consequences of using abusive behavior are explored, such as court and jail experience and the impact the abusive incident had on significant others in their life, i.e., partners, children or parents. Men are asked to self-evaluate the degree to which they feel

Figure 2
Interventions and stages of change and group development

Interventions	Group Stage [1]	Anticipated level of individual motivation for change

1. Make organizational decision about use of involuntary group.
2. Pre-group orientation
  a. Initial orientation of group
  b. Anticipate resistance and reframe as ambivalence.
  c. Clarify and validate choices
3. Emphasize joining and inclusion
  a. Clarify non-negotiables.
  b. Support positive choices made to date.
  c. Provide emotional support
  d. Identify self-motivating statements.
  e. Provide opening statement addressing client concerns/fears.
  f. Stimulate non-threatening attention to issues.
  g. Support self-evaluation regarding possible problem.
  h. Review formal testing to provides information on potential problem.
  i. Reframe resistance as ambivalence.
  j. Continue to clarify non-negotiables
  k. Continue to clarify choices
	Pre-group planning
	
	Beginning
		Pre-contemplation

4. Deciding to make a change
  a. Assist in assessing costs and benefits of change
  b. Provide information about choices
  c. Provide videos that dramatize the consequences of not changing.
	Middle	Contemplation

5. Support in planning actions; preparation for action, i.e., role-play, buddy systems. 6. Gather feedback on change attempts.		Preparation Action
7. Utilize clear criteria for group completion a. Plan for maintenance; Prepare for lapse via role-play.	Ending	Maintenance

(Adopted from Rooney and Chovanec, 2004)

1 Kurland and SalmonModel of Group Development (1998)

responsible for the abusive incident. Including other group members in the discussion who may be further ahead in the change process is useful as they many times, can identify with the men who do not see a problem and can offer ideas that helped them in the change process, i.e., talking to others and taking responsibility for self. The following is an example of work with a pre-contemplator in an early session:

Joe is a 27 year old who has been in and out of chemical dependency treatment. He reports that he was charged with fifth degree assault when he and his partner of several years got into an argument over an old boyfriend who they had seen at the bar that night. Joe reports they were both drunk and the argument escalated to Joe shoving his partner, which he claims he had no other choice. 'I was trying to get her out of my face.' She promptly called police. Joe and his partner are no longer together.

Joe: 'I don't know why I am here. She is the one that needs an anger program. Besides I am no longer with her and I have not drunk since this happened so this problem will never happen again. I don't consider myself to have an anger problem.'

Leader: 'Sounds like you are feeling forced into being here (Reflective skills). Given that you have come tonight tells me that at least part of you wants to figure out what happened to make sure it never happens again (Assuming ambivalence). A lot of men decide not to attend this group and go to jail instead so I support your choice (Validate choice to attend treatment). Even if you don't re-connect with this partner you want to make sure this type of situation doesn't happen (Possible client goal). Looking back on the incident what part do you take responsibility for from 0% to 100%? (Encourage self-evaluation) Sounds like this argument caught you off guard and that things happened pretty quickly.'

Joe: 'I take maybe 40% responsibility for what happened. I did shove her, but she forced me to do it.'

Leader: 'Joe, it takes courage to take responsibility for your part in the past conflict. That 40% is what we will focus in on in this program since that is the part that you have control of. Who else in this group can identify with the struggle to take responsibility for their part in past abuse?' (Linking other men farther ahead in the change process.)

Another group member: It is very hard to take responsibility especially when your partner gets you mad. It took me along time before I acknowledged my part in our battles.

Contemplators may also be present in the beginning of group as earlier research suggests (O'Hare, 1996). The focus in domestic abuse treatment is on exploring the pros and cons of ending abusive behavior. Contemplators are encouraged to self-evaluate on the consequences of continuing abusive behavior, like the effects of anger on ones physical health or the impact of their children witnessing the abuse. Videos that dramatize the impact of abuse on victims and their family members are also useful when men are in this stage. The goal is to help the client resolve their ambivalence about ending abusive behavior. The facilitator supports any attempts at change and helps them evaluate them. Group members again are extremely helpful providing information on the impact of abusive behavior and how they went about resolving their ambivalence towards the problem. The following is an example of work with a contemplator in an early session:

Joe: 'After a few sessions I have decided that I can't do anything about that court order now so I might as well make the most out of it. I still think my ex-partner should have a group like this but I know I did shove her. I am realizing that I was a jerk at times. Things just started building up and when she got in my face and told me she didn't love me anymore I couldn't handle it.'

Leader: 'It takes a lot of courage to look at oneself and take responsibility. What helped you do this? Sounds like you want to make sure this type of incident doesn't happen again. Tell me more about how things started to build up. What things can you do to avoid this type of build up in the future? What would pull you back into experiencing that type of pressure again?' (Examining pros/cons).

Joe: 'I had a bad day at work with my boss giving me a hard time. When I got home I started to get upset with the little things she said and before you know it we were screaming at each other. It happened so quickly. I'm not sure what I can do to avoid the pressure build up. All I know is that I don't want to ever experience that again.'

Leader: 'How many men can identify with Joe's pattern of getting angry? What have others done to deal with this pattern? The challenge is how to speak up without putting others down before things get out of hand.' (Linking to other group members who have addressed this pattern of anger build up.)

Middle stage

In the middle group stage, with the earlier efforts of engaging men in the change process, you will have men in the preparation and action stage of change. The stage fits well with a majority of teaching interventions identified in a traditional domestic abuse program. For example, the Duluth model identifies one of the roles of the facilitator is that of providing information on relationship skills and encouraging critical and reflective thinking (Pence & Paymar, 1993). Teaching counter conditioning, finding alternatives to abusive behavior is focused on in this stage, as well as offering reflective listening skills and 'I messages' to improve communication in relationships. Role-play and modeling behavior is useful in building men's confidence to try out skills/information learned in the group. The goal of the facilitator is to support change efforts of the men and encourage self-evaluation and feedback from others to help refine their efforts to change. Daniel & Murphy (1997) encourage the use of 'buddy' systems for social support as men try out various change efforts among their family and friends when men are in the action stage.

Ending stage

In the ending group stage most men are building confidence in changing their abusive behaviors and are ready to examine ways of maintaining their changes after group is completed. On a program level it is important that there are clear criteria for treatment completion, i.e., number of tasks/sessions. This not only reduces reactance of men entering the program but also provides clear feedback to participants about their progress in the group. Clear criteria for program completion also is helpful to partners, family and probation workers who are interested in the participants progress.

Relapse is a particular dangerous problem in domestic abuse treatment as it leads to re-assault of partners. In a review of 25 studies post treatment re-assault was found to be 36% (Rosenfeld, 1992). Given these safety concerns more attention to relapse prevention is in order. Useful relapse prevention strategies have been developed for domestic abuse treatment (Jennings, 1990). Daniel and Murphy (1997) make a distinction in domestic abuse treatment between a 'lapse' that results in verbal and psychological abuse and a relapse that results in a re-assault.

They recommend focusing on lapses in men's change efforts to reduce the risk of relapse. Men can be asked to identify situations that test their ability to be non-abusive. Once these situations are identified men can brainstorm alternative strategies with the group to reduce their risk of becoming verbally or psychologically abusive, which can lead to physical assault. Also requiring that men connect outside the group for a series of meetings to discuss ways to maintain their changes can be helpful. The intent of the meetings is to increase the chance of men using former group members as support as they run into challenges once they have completed the program.

Research implications

As a result of the safety concerns of women, it is understandable that early research in domestic abuse treatment focused on the extent programs extinguished physical abuse and reduced emotional abuse of abusers. However, given the attrition problem, more focus needs to be placed on how abusive men engage in the treatment process. While the frameworks of stages of change, motivational interviewing and reactance theory appear promising in reducing the attrition problem, further research on programs that implement them are needed. For example, while evidence is building that pre-contemplators are common in mental health clients (McConnaughy et al., 1989), alcohol abuse (DeClemente and Hughes, 1990), cocaine abuse and juvenile delinquency (Prochaska et al., 1994), little is know about the readiness for change in domestic abuse clients. The Stages of Change Scale (McConnaughy et al., 1989; O'Hare, 1996) used to assess stages of change in the above populations could easily be used with men entering domestic abuse treatment. While high reactance has been confirmed in a sample of men entering domestic abuse treatment (Chovanec, 1995), further exploration is needed to assess reactance levels as men progress through treatment.

Practice implications for groupwork

The application of reactance theory, stages of change and motivational interviewing to domestic abuse treatment needs to be considered in the context of a community response to ending domestic violence. These innovations are considered program components that enhance men's engagement with treatment. The goals of treatment, including ending physical and emotional abuse and getting men to take responsibility for their abusive behavior, remain the same as those identified in traditional domestic abuse programs. However, accomplishing these goals are attempted by challenging men when they are more likely to accept it, better pacing interventions to match men's readiness for change. This has major implications for group work practice. Assessing reactance levels and stages of change as men enter a program allow group facilitators to better gauge the social pressures men enter a program with and their readiness for change. Facilitators are better able to anticipate initial resistance men present and move them sequentially along the change process. This means for those in pre-contemplation, a group facilitator only needs to move men towards contemplation, considering the possibility of change. Once in contemplation, the goal is to examine both sides of the ambivalence to change. Once in preparation small change efforts are identified and supported. The terms 'court-order' or 'involuntary' no longer needs to be considered a static process that needs to be confronted. Group facilitators are more likely to identify those men farther ahead in the change process and can assist others movement towards change, particularly in open-ended groups. Finally, better use of the change process within group facilitation allows for the channeling of anger and hostility men present early in treatment toward client change rather than directed toward confrontational interventions that increase the risk of dropout and can lead to group facilitator burn-out and continued abuse.

Hopefully with better pacing with men in the change process treatment attrition can be reduced and the primary goal of ending physical abuse and reducing emotional abuse achieved. The hope is that these alternative approaches provide a more respectful and human way of achieving them. The men, their partners and children, and the larger community all serve to benefit.

References

Austin, J.B., and Dankwort, J. (1999). Standards for batterer programs: A review end analysts. *Journal of Interpersonal Violence, 14*, 152-168.

Beutler, L..E. and Berren, M. (Eds.). (1995). *Intergrative assessment of adult personality.* New York: Guilford.

Beutler, L..E., Kim, E.J., Davidson, E., Karno, M. and Fisher, D. (1996). Research contributions to improving managed health care outcomes. *Psychotherapy, 33*, 197-206.

Brehm, S. and Brehm, J. (1981). *Psychological reactance: A theory of freedom and control.* New York: Academic Press Inc.

Brekke, J. (1989). The use of orientation groups for hard-to-reach clients: Model, method and evaluation. *Social Work with Groups, 12(2)*, 75-88.

Cadsky, O., Hanson, R.K., Crawford, M. and Lalonde, C. (1996). Attrition from a male batterer treatment program: Client-treatment congruence and lifestyle instability. *Violence and Victims,11(1)*, 51-64.

Caplan, T. and Thomas, H. (1995). Safety and comfort, content and process: Facilitating open group work with men who batter. *Social Work with Groups, 18*, 33-51.

Caplan, T. and Thomas, H. (2002). 'The Forgotten Moment: Therapeutic resiliency and its promotion in social work with groups.' *Social Work with Groups, 24(2)*, 5-26.

Chovanec, Michael G. (1995). Attrition in the Treatment of Men Who Batter: A Closer Look at Men's Decision-Making Process About Attending or Dropping Out of Treatment. *Proceedings of the Eighth National Symposium on Doctoral Research and Social Work Practice*, The Ohio State University, November 3-4.

Daly, J.E. and Pelowski S.(2000). Predictors of dropout among men who batter: A review of studies with implications for research and practice. Violence and Victims, *15(2)*, 137-160.

Daniels, J.W. and Murphy, C.M. (1997). Stages and processes of change in batterers' treatment, *Cognitive and Behavioral Practice. 4(1)*, 123-145.

Davis, R. Taylor, B. and Maxwell, C. (1998). *Does batterer treatment reduce violence? A randomized experiment in Brooklyn.* Washington, DC: National Institute of Justice.

DeHart, D.D., Kennerly, R.J., Burke, L.K. and Follingstad, D.R. (1999). Predictors of attrition in a treatment program for battering men. *Journal of Family Violence, 14(1)*, 19-34.

DeMaris, A. (1989). Attrition in batterers' counseling: The role of social and demographic factors. *Social Service Review, 63*, March, 142-154.

Dutton, D.G. (1986). The outcome of court-mandated treatment for wife assault: A quasi-experimental evaluation. *Violence and Victims, 1,* 163-175.

Dutton, D.G. and Starzomski, A.J. (1993). Borderline personality in perpetrators of psychological and physical abuse. Violence and Victims, 8, 327-337.

DiClemente, C.C. and Hughes, S.O. (1990). Stages of change profiles in outpatient alcoholism treatment. Journal of Substance Abuse, 2, 217-235.

Edleson, J.L. and Grusznski, R.J. (1988). Treating men who batter: Four years of outcome data from the Domestic Abuse Project. *Journal of Social Service Research, 12,* 1, 3-22.

Edleson, J.L. and Syers, M. (1989). *Domestic Abuse Project research update (No.2),* Minneapolis MN: Domestic Abuse Project, Inc.

Edleson, J.L. and Toman, R.M.(1992). Intervention for men who batter, An ecological approach. Sage Publications. New Berry Park: CA.

Eisikovits, Z.C. and Edleson, J.L. (1989). Intervening with men who batter: A critical review of the literature. *Social Service Review, 37,* 385-414.

Faulkner, K. K., Cogan, R., Nolder, M. and Shooter, G. (1991). Characteristics of men and women completing cognitive-behavioral spouse abuse treatment. *Journal of Family Violence, 6(3),* 243-254.

Feder, L. and Forde, D. (2000). *A test of the efficacy of court-mandated counseling for domestic violence offenders: The Broward experiment.* Washington, DC: National Institute of Justice.

Gondolf, E.W. (1988). The Effects of Batterer Counseling on Shelter Outcome. Journal of Interpersonal Violence, 3(3), 275-289.

Gondolf, E.W. (1991). A victim-based assessment of court-mandated counseling for batterers. Criminal Justice Review, 16, 214-226.

Gondolf, E.W. (1997). Expanding batterer program evaluation. In G.K. Kantor and J. Jasinski (Eds.), Out of darkness: Contemporary research perspectives on family violence. Thousand Oaks, CA: Sage.

Gondolf, E.W. (1997b). Batterer Programs, What we know and need to know. *Journal of Interpersonal Violence, 12(1),* 83-98.

Gondolf, E.W. (1997c). Patterns of reassault in batterers programs. *Violence and Victims, 12,* 373-387.

Gondolf, E.W. (1999). A comparison of reassault rates in four batterer programs: Do court referral, program length, and services matter? *Journal of Interpersonal Violence, 14,* 41-61.

Gondolf, E.W. (2000). A 30-month follow-up of court-referred batterers in four cities. *International Journal of Offender Therapy and Comparative Criminology, 44(1),* 111-128.

Gondolf, E.W. (2001). Current hot topics, Limitations of experimental evaluation of batterer programs. *Trauma, Violence and Abuse, 2(1),* 79-88.

Gondolf, E.W. and Foster, B. (1991). Preprogram attrition in batterer programs. *Journal of Family Violence, 6,* 337-349.

Groth-Marnat, G. (1997). *Handbook of psychological assessment (3rd Ed.).* New York: Wiley.

Hagen, M. A. (1998, July). Bad attitude. *National Review, 50,* Issue 13, 38-39.

Hamberger, L.K. and Hastings, J.E. (1989). Counseling male spouse abusers: Characteristics of treatment completers and dropouts. *Violence and Victims, 4,* 275-286.

Hamberger, L.K., Lohr, J.M. and Gottlieb, M. (2000). Predictors of treatment dropout from spouse abuse abatement program. *Behavior Modification, 24(4),* 528-552.

Hamberger, L.K. and Hastings, J.E. (1991). Personality correlates of men who batter and nonviolent men: Some continuities and discontinuities. *Journal of Family* Violence, *6,* 131-147.

Healey, K., Smith, C., and O'Sullivan, C. (1998). Batter intervention: Program approaches and criminal justice strategies. Issues and Practices in Criminal Justice. Washington, D.C.: National Institute of Justice.

Howard, M.O. and Jenson, J.M. (1999). Clinical practice guidelines: Should social work develop them? Research on Social Work Practice, *9(3),* 283-301.

Howard, M.O., Edmond, T. and Vaughn, M.G. (2005). Mental health practice guidelines: Panacea or Pipedream? In S. Kirk (Ed.), *Mental disorders in the social environment: Critical perspectives.* Columbia University Press.

Jennings, J.L. (1987). History and Issues in the Treatment of Battering Men: A Case for Unstructured Group Therapy. *Journal of Family Violence, 2(3),* 193-213.

Jennings, J.L. (1990). Preventing Relapse Versus 'Stopping' Domestic Abuse Violence: Do We Expect Too Much Too Soon From Battering Men? *Journal of Family Violence, 5(1),* 43-60.

Lambert, M.J. and Bergin, A.E. (1994). The effectiveness of psychotherapy. In A.E. Bergin and S.I. Garfield (Eds.), *Handbook of psychotherapy and behavior change* (4th Ed., pp.143-189). New York: John Wiley.

McConnaughy, E.A., DiClemente, C.C., Prochaska, J.O. and Velicer, W.F. (1989). Stages of change in psychotherapy: A follow-up report. *Psychotherapy, 26,* 494-503.

Miller, Ted et al. (1996). *Victim Costs and Consequences: A New Look.* National Institute of Justice, U.S. Department of Justice, 18-19.

Miller, W.R. (1985). Motivation for treatment: A review with special emphasis on alcoholism. *Psychological Bulletin, 98,* 84-107.

Miller, W.R. and Rollnick, S. (1991). Motivational Interviewing, Preparing People to Change Addictive Behavior. The Guilford Press: New York.

Murphy, C.M. and Baxter, V.A. (1997). Motivating batterers to change in the treatment context. *Journal of Interpersonal Violence, 12(4)*, 607-619.

Norcross, J.C., Beutler, L.E. and Clarkin, J.F. (1998). Prescriptive Eclectic Psychotherapy (Ch. 11) *Paradigms of Clinical Social Work (Vol. 2)*, R. A. Dorfman (Ed.), Brunner/Mazel Publishers: New York.

O'Hare, T. (1996). Court-ordered versus Voluntary Clients: Problem Differences and Readiness for Change in *Social Work, 41(4)*, 417-422.

Palmer, S.E., Brown, R.A. and Barrera, M.E. (1992). Group treatment program for abusive husbands: Long-term evaluation. *American Journal of Orthopsychiatry, 62(2)*, 276-283.

Pence, E. and Paymar, M. (1993). Education groups for men who batter: The Duluth model. New York: Springer.

Pirog-Good, M. and Stets-, J. (1985). Male batterers and battering prevention programs: A national survey. *Response, 9*, 8-12.

Prochaska, J.O., DiClemente, C.C. and Norcross, J.C. (1992). In search of how people change: Application to addictive behaviors. *American Psychologist, 47*, 1102-1114.

Prochaska J.O., Velicer, W.F., Rossi, J.S., Goldstein, M.G., Marcus, B.H., Rakowski, W., Fiore, C., Harlow, L.L., Redding, C.A., Rosenbloom, D. and Rossi, S.R. (1994). Stages of change and decisional balance for twelve problem behaviors. *Health Psychology, 13*, 39-46

Prochaska, J., Norcross, J. and DiClemente, C. (1994). *Changing for Good.* Avon Books: New York, New York

Roberts, A.R. (1998). *Battered women and their families: Intervention strategies and treatment approaches (2nd ed.).* New York: Springer

Rollnick, S. and Morgan, M. (1995). Motivational interviewing: Increasing readiness for change (Chapter 9). *Psychotherapy and Substance Abuse: A Practitioner's Handbook,* A. Washton (Ed.), The Guildford Press: New York, 179-191

Rooney, R.H. (1992). *Strategies for work with involuntary clients.* New York: Columbia University Press

Rooney, R.H. and Chovanec, M.. (2004). Social Work with Involuntary Groups. *Handbook of Social Work with Groups,* Edited by C.D. Garvin, M.J. Galinsky andL.M. Gutierrez. Guilford Publications Inc

Rosenfeld B. (1992). Court-ordered treatment of spouse abuse. *Clinical Psychology Review, 12*, 205-226

Saunders, D. (1996). Feminist-cognitive-behavioral and process-psychodynamic treatments for men who batter: Interaction of abuser traits and treatment models. *Violence and Victims, 11*, 393-414

Shupe, A., Stacey, W.A. and Hazelwood, L.R. (1987). *Violent men, violent couples* Lexington, MA: Lexington Books

Stosny, S. (1994). Shadows of the heart: A dramatic video for the treatment resistance of spouse abusers. *Social Work, 39* (6), 686-694

Thomas, E.J. and Yoshioka, M.R. (1989). Spouse intervention confrontations in unilateral family therapy for alcohol abuse. *Social Casework: The Journal of Contemporary* Social Work, *70,* 340-347

Thomas, H. and Caplan, T. (1999). Spinning the group process wheel: Effective facilitation techniques for motivating involuntary client groups. *Social Work with Groups, 2* (4), 3-21

Tolman R and Bennett, L. (1990). A review of quantitative research on men who batter. *Journal of Interpersonal Violence, 5,* 87-118

Tolman, R.M. and Bhosley, G. (1987). A comparison of two types of pregroup preparation for men who batter. In *The Third Symposium for the Empirical foundations of Group Work,* Symposium conducted in May, Chicago, Illinois

3

'I have a dream':

A visioning group for adolescent First Nations girls

Arielle Dylan

Girls in North American society grow up in what Pipher (1994) aptly terms a 'girl poisoning' culture. While adolescence involves significant developmental and physical changes for children (Erikson, 1968), struggles for identity can be more challenging for girls because they are burdened with enormous societal and cultural pressures to abandon their true selves (Kilbourne, 1990). Coming of age in a misogynistic culture in which men, especially white men, continue to possess most of the political and economic power, silences girls' voices. Even though feminism and the women's liberation movement have created more opportunities for young North American women, the most powerful contemporary message from society and the media is that a young woman's purpose is to please others by becoming a commodity, and/ or by being beautiful, self-sacrificing, passive and caring. Simone de Beauvoir (1953) asserts that adolescence marks the start of a struggle for self-definition in a culture that confines women's primary identity to that of passive object for male interest. Within these narrow parameters, pre-adolescent and adolescent girls will often stifle healthy impulses rather than risk flouting the culturally scripted female role. Girls will sometimes starve themselves for the sake of approximating the pervasive beauty ideal, or focus on being pretty and pleasing rather than athletic and strong minded, or be polite and other-oriented rather than honest and self aware. This struggle with forming an identity in a patriarchal, sexist, image-based, media-obsessed culture has an injurious impact on girls' physical, emotional and mental well-being. Social critics and psychologists have identified a higher incidence in a range of problems afflicting pre-adolescent and adolescent girls in recent years, including low self-esteem, drug and alcohol issues, eating disorders, sexually transmitted diseases, unusual phobias (for example, fear of attending school), self harming behaviours, and suicide attempts (Gilligan et al., 1991; Kilbourne, 2003; Pipher, 1994).

The 'I Have a Dream' (IHD) project is a model designed to empower pre-adolescent and adolescent girls, helping them maintain their authentic selves in a culture where mass communication peddles harmful values and superficial, unattainable standards. The girls' group developed in direct response to volunteer experiences with girls on a northern Ontario reserve, client need being the cornerstone upon which the group structure was built (Northen and Kurland, 2001). Statements made by many of the girls with whom I was volunteering, revealed that they had no dreams for their future, nor did they have any ideas about what they wanted to do when they finished high school. In an effort to counteract the devastating effects of media-saturated, girl-silencing Western culture, this strengths-based, empowerment project aimed to help girls maintain (or regain) their authentic selves in the difficult, transitional, identity-forming period of adolescence. Using an education and career-pursuit framework, the group was meant to empower pre-adolescent and adolescent females to reject deleterious dominant cultural messages and make decisions based on personal interests and self-knowledge (Bowling et al., 2000).

Context

We understand, through gender scholarship, that education must provide more than equal programming to counter the larger cultural and social forces affecting the development of girls (Heilman, 1998). On the cusp of adolescence, girls evidence signs of diminished voice, often developing a new reluctance to discuss ideas and share feelings. Girls 'lose a sense of authority about their experience and knowledge and are more willing to trust the knowledge and experience of others' (Dorney, 1995, p. 58). This loss of voice and confidence occurs at a critical developmental time when the experience of ability and personal strength should be enlarging (Heilman, 1998). Current research indicates that powerful cultural and social messages undermine girls' self regard as they enter their adolescent years (Spira et al., 2002).

Sadly, research also demonstrates that being physically attractive surpasses having ability as the most important determining factor of schoolgirls' self-worth (AAUW, 1991). In their endeavours to achieve the ubiquitous beauty myth trafficked mercilessly by media and corporatism, girls commodify themselves, placing primacy on appearance at the expense of important, integral dimensions of their self. Under these conditions, many girls do not reach their human, academic or professional potential.

First Nations girls not only struggle with all these issues but also with the marginalization and racism that mainstream media and Western cultural values perpetuate. The history of First Nations-European relations in Canada is one of institutional racism at the political, educational and religious levels, fuelled by systematic attempts to eradicate, and later, to assimilate First Nations (Miller, 1996; RCAP, 1996). From the late nineteenth century to the late twentieth century, First Nations children were removed from their parents and their traditional ways. They were forced to enter residential schools and forbidden to speak their native languages under threat of corporal punishment (McKenzie et al., 1995; Miller, 1996; LaRocque, 1996). This mandatory dislocation effectively fractured family unity and the kinship network, destroying communities, damaging culture, and obliterating many First Nations languages (LaForme, 1991). The extent of cultural decimation is incalculable and the impact of colonialism and its consequent multigenerational trauma is apparent today on reserves and in national statistics: First Nations people have the nation's shortest life expectancy; highest rates of suicide, unemployment, poverty, and infant mortality; and are over-represented in institutions of incarceration (Frideres, 1996; RCAP, 1996; Durst, 1992).

It is true that most of the rooftops at the reserve where this group took place were adorned with satellite dishes, and many of the children and youth have adopted Eurocentric and hip-hop mannerisms and styles of dress, but this does not suggest an absence of cultural dissonance. The infiltration of dominant culture programming and values can negatively impact First Nations (for example, see Mander's (1991) discussion of the havoc wreaked on a Dene community as the result of the introduction of satellite dishes); engendering feelings of inferiority, and possibly reinforcing already internalized racism and stereotypes. The stereotype of the 'squaw,' a most pernicious stereotype suggesting First Nations women and girls are lustful, immoral, unfeeling and dirty (LaRocque, 1996) has rendered them vulnerable to physical, psychological and sexual violence (RCAP, 1996). While bicultural contexts are sometimes thought to safeguard girls from pernicious media forces, television programming featuring females primarily from the dominant culture could negatively impact First Nations girls, reinscribing the squaw stereotype through otherness. Centuries of racist practices committed by the dominant culture have marginalized First Nations people, and First Nations girls in patriarchal Western culture are further marginalized by their gender. The distrust of and disinclination from Eurocentric educational institutions, and the concerns about succeeding in such settings, are very understandable for First Nations girls who face the twin structural barriers of racism and sexism in the dominant culture.

Group work as a modality

Group work has been a long-standing, potent intervention in the history of social work. Malekoff (1997) has elucidated the appropriateness and effectiveness of group work with vulnerable persons, a category highly pertinent to girls during the identity-threatening onset of adolescence. Further, several girls in the IHD group were vulnerable because of specific risk factors with which they were contending, such as poverty, isolation, family substance abuse, and other forms of family stress. Of interest for the IHD project are those groups that used a peer-support, strengths-based, empowerment approach. In the past few years, numerous successful programs have been developed involving any one or combination of these methods, demonstrating model effectiveness, and utilizing client strength and resilience. Walsh-Burke and Scanlon's (2000) 'Beyond Reviving Ophelia,' a psycho-educational group for mothers and daughters is an excellent example of a strengths-based program, achieving repeated positive qualitative results. 'Empower,' the feminist consciousness-raising curriculum for adolescent women, developed by Bowling et al. (2000), is a strong empowerment model emphasizing 'self-knowledge, self-esteem, assertive communication, relationship violence, body image, sexual decision-making, career exploration, and self-care' (p. 3). Participants' responses were positive, with reports of increased knowledge of self and influences of societal messages. Azzarto's (1997) young women's support group, using a holistic approach to prevention that encouraged the formation of healthy relationships in a supportive environment, provided participants room to explore and develop ideas, become more self-aware and enhance self-esteem. Groups have been used traditionally in the feminist movement as a form of consciousness-raising; when the personal is political, the collective becomes the ideal locus for comprehending the insidious and systemic nature of the experienced oppression. During the developmental stage of adolescence, 'parents have limited influence .... As daughters move into the broader culture, they care what their friends, not their parents, think' (Pipher, 1994, p. 38). Through increasing time spent in peer relationships, adolescents gain a variety of social experiences and further develop their interpersonal skills (Northen and Kurland, 2001). There is a unique parlance that adolescents typically possess, establishing 'them as a developmental cohort...distinguishable from adults and young children' (Rose, 1998). Clearly, the dynamism of peer interactions and the opportunities for mutuality makes group work highly suited to social work programs involving adolescents.

The IHD model

This strengths-based, empowerment-focused, support-group model was developed by the author to help girls (ages 11 to 14) navigate the tempestuous currents of adolescence and hold onto an intact, authentic self. Two compatible frameworks undergird this program: cultivation theory and feminist theory. Cultivation theory suggests that relentless media exposure can alter an individual's beliefs about social reality and influence gender role attitudes and behaviour (Gerbner et al., 1993; Signorielli and Morgan, 1990). Cultivation theory is especially appropriate because, unlike social learning or social comparison theory, this approach de-emphasizes the individual, placing primacy on the role of sociostructural forces rather than personal responses. Feminist theory is important to this project for its ability to meet squarely the obvious juncture between sexism and patriarchy, the silencing of girls' voices and the attack on their authentic selves through social, cultural and media messages that are emblematic of the hegemonic, patriarchal system. Feminist theory is the organizing principle of this project, a group intervention that encourages member agency while promoting consciousness-raising and self-regard (Cox, 1991; Saulnier, 2000).

> By emphasizing an ethic of mutuality and interdependency feminist thinking offers us a way to end domination while simultaneously changing the impact of inequality. (hooks, 2000, p. 117)

The primary goal of this group is to assist girls in the defence of their authentic self through the theme of educational and career pursuit. The related objectives are several:

1. to increase assertiveness, self-esteem, self-empowerment, and a sense of competency;
2. to celebrate girl/womanhood, have networking opportunities, promote critical thinking and build community; and
3. to challenge patriarchy and resist internalization of its values, identify and resist persistent colonial forces, and encourage the discovery and pursuit of true passions. To evaluate the progress of members, summary reports were made at the end of each group to trace changes in attitudes, relationships and behaviours (Northen and Kurland, 2001).

We hope that this project, through providing a positive focus, will counter the problems of loneliness, low self-esteem, disordered eating, self-harming behaviour, abusive relationships, violence, unwanted pregnancy, and risky decision-making (pertaining to drug and alcohol use, and sexual activity) that many girls struggle with during adolescence. In this way, the IHD project also functions as a prevention and intervention group where the exposure to options, opportunities and life-affirming possibilities enables girls to choose to move toward something positive (e.g., educational and career goals), rather than simply avoiding something potentially negative (e.g., illicit drug use).

The program idea and model was presented to the Director of the Native Child Welfare (NCW) agency on the reserve. She believed it was a worthy project and approved funding the group through the Youth Activities and Addiction Prevention program, which had a coordinator who was also in strong support. Along with the budget, NCW generously granted use of the fully fuelled agency van, as well as stationery and other supplies. The NCW director and I decided that the project would be made accessible to all girls on the reserve between the ages of eleven and fourteen, membership would not exceed eight participants, and enrolment would be based on order of response.

The decision to limit the group to eight members was based on there being only one facilitator (myself) who would eventually be taking the girls on field trips. Initial concerns about having to refuse interested girls wanting to enrol once the group was full were relieved when only seven girls had signed up by the enrolment closing date. However, once participants began sharing experiences and group adventures with non-members, I learned that several more girls wanted to join the group. Because the project is highly task oriented, involving significant scheduling, it was decided at the outset the group should be closed.

Schematically, the project was designed as a time limited structured group, a ten-session model delivered in two parts. Phase one of the project required the girls to consider and research future educational and career pursuits of interest, while phase two comprised field trips to educational institutions of the participants' choice within the province of Ontario. By the fourth week, each participant was to have selected the program she would like to investigate at either a trade, college or university institution. With this information I contacted their chosen post-secondary institutions and arranged each girls' 'Dream Day' to include an information session and tour of the educational department, and a related experiential component. Together the girls would participate in each other's dreams through the researching, planning, and excursion elements.

The first session began with an ice-breaking exercise to engage the girls in a fun activity and ease any initial discomfort. This was followed by having the girls establish ground rules for the group to promote a safe environment. The participants generated an impressive and thoughtful list of guidelines, leaving out one seemingly important rule regarding attire. When I mentioned dress, the girls quickly shared that they had to follow a dress code at school and figured they should apply the same code in this education-oriented girls' group. After explaining the purpose and structure of the program, three texts were distributed: Martin Luther King's famous and inspirational 'I Have a Dream' speech, and excerpts from talks given by former Grand Chief Matthew Coon Come, and writer and activist Gloria Steinem. The three handouts underscored the themes of knowing one's self, having faith in oneself, and pursuing one's dreams. Each member was also given a journal and a pen, so she could chronicle her thoughts, ideas, feelings, and aspirations while participating in this visioning journey. Members were told that they were not expected to share journal entries, but the journal might serve to remind them of meaningful events and help them clarify and explore thoughts and feelings that may arise during the group experience (Stone, 1998). In much the same way that narrative practice helps individuals gain control of their lives through re-authoring their narratives (Abels and Abels, 2002), the act of journaling symbolizes our storied existence, providing a site for reflection and critical thinking, resistance and change.

Sessions two and three were research focused and took place at a nearby off-reserve library. Time had been booked in advance to use the computers and Internet service, and the girls began investigating trade, college and university programs. I circulated, helping all the girls with their searches and began to notice the beginnings of group agency and peer support as the girls assisted each other with the research process and encouraged each other's interests. The affiliative dynamic appeared early in the group (Schiller, 1997), leading to an intimacy that was present throughout the remaining sessions. Unlike the standard format of group development outlined by Garland et al. (1965), the group progressed from the first meeting's pre-affiliation stage to quickly 'establishing a relational base' by the second and third meetings, where members spent a considerable amount of time comparing notes and discussing 'Dream Day' choices (Schiller, 2003). Moreover, mutual-aid was apparent in the early stages of group development as members began to share strengths and exhibit a sense of purposeful use of self while engaged in the common purpose of conceptualizing, designing and pursuing their outings. The structural decentralization of authority inherent in the group design, through having each member author her own 'Dream Day,' helped to create a 'forum for mutual aid' (Steinberg, 2004, p. 163).

Three of the girls were certain of what they wanted to study; for them, it was a matter of finding the most suitable and appealing program. The remaining four girls had several areas of interest, and they used the process of exploring educational and training programs to narrow their career choices and select the option that seemed to fit the best. Of course, with the girls being between 11 and 14 years of age, their career interests will likely change by the time they enter post-secondary institutions; but in this program the process of engaging in future planning required that the girls reach into themselves and inquire as to who they are and what interests them. This is the process of self-examination, which leads to self-knowledge, a buffer against the inescapable toxic mainstream cultural environment. The fourth session was a dinner and discussion meeting in which the girls delivered their choices to me and shared with the group their interests. It was during this session that the group cohesion became apparent

(Northen and Kurland, 2001). The girls had come to think of themselves as a group, and they requested an extra outing that would occur after all member field trips were completed. While showing an interest in the suggestion, I indicated uncertainty about the budget being able to cover the extra expense. The girls, in their enthusiasm, began talking about fundraising through holding a car wash and other events. In the end, with the remaining budget and a donation from the community's Economic Development, there was enough money for an extra and final trip, and the girls consensually decided on the destination.

After contacting and speaking with department heads at the selected programs and institutions and scheduling all the visits, the next several weeks involved travelling to colleges and universities so each girl could have her Dream Day. In speaking with department representatives and coordinators, I mentioned the girls are First Nations, and requested, where possible, that they have an opportunity to meet with First Nations students, teachers, and professionals during the outings. With the existing structural barriers to First Nations students entering institutions of higher learning (Wood and Clay, 1996), I did not want the excursions to be marked by an absence and invisibility of First Nations adults. Given the reality of race and racism and the truth of white privilege, I did not want the girls to feel alienated by First Nations invisibility and conclude that they do not belong (hooks, 2000). Moreover, First Nations people studying and teaching at institutions of higher learning would be excellent role models for the group. Of the seven group members, we had individuals interested in theatre arts, law, music, theology, and fashion design. Five of the seven girls had chosen to visit schools in Toronto, including the University of Toronto, York University, Osgoode Hall Law School, and Ryerson University. Unfortunately, due to the SARS epidemic, the reserve's Chief and Council passed a Band Council Resolution forbidding all programs to take participants to Toronto until the health risks had abated. The five Toronto trips had to be abandoned, and I was, in a short time, faced with the task of finding similar substitute programs at institutions outside the city of Toronto. Once everything was rescheduled, we began our outings.

The following example illustrates the bipartite informative and experiential structure of the field trips. One of the girls who plans to study law in the future had decided she wanted to visit Western University's Law School. The morning of this trip the IHD girls' group had a meeting at the Law Faculty where we met with the Dean of the Law School, the admissions officer, a First Nations law professor, and the departmental coordinator who had arranged the meeting. After this information session, a third-year law student gave us a tour of the law building, introducing us to other law students who were doing research in a variety of areas. We broke for lunch, and in the afternoon we visited the city courthouse. The Manager of Courthouse Operations had set up a meeting, held in one of the courtrooms, for the IHD group with a First Nations Justice of the Peace and a First Nations lawyer. During this discussion, two First Nations court workers joined us to share information about their work, and answer any questions we might have. When we had finished meeting with the Justice of the Peace and the girls had asked all their pre-prepared and impromptu questions, the two court workers took us into a courtroom that was in session. The girls had a powerful experience of learning about the academic aspect of law in an educational setting, coupled with the application of law in a professional setting. The impact of interacting with several First Nations legal professionals was considerable. One of the IHD members commented, 'That JP's from a small reserve. If he can do it so can I.'

Throughout the field trips there was evidence of 'mutuality and interpersonal empathy' (Schiller, 2003), as members connected with each other's 'Dream Days' by preparing questions to ask departmental representatives, being genuinely interested in each member's outing, and offering support to members who felt unsure of their group input. Although each member chose to explore a distinct, post-secondary program of study, members demonstrated an appreciation of these differences while maintaining a strong relational base. For example, one member who was going to be visiting a department of music was very excited about another member's opportunity to visit a fashion design program, helping the member interested in fashion to sketch clothing designs she could present on her 'Dream Day.' Such group member interactions revealed a process of co-dreaming, palpably underscoring the phenomenon of 'groupness' (Middleman and Wood, 1990).

When we had completed our educational field trips, we went on our fun trip that the girls had requested. This was an overnight trip beginning with a drive through the African Lion Safari, followed by an evening and the next day in Niagara Falls. Both sites were educational in a non-academic way, and allowed the girls to have fun together as a collective while still processing the tremendous learning that had occurred through their visioned Dream Days. The importance and role of fun throughout all the trips and meetings deserves special consideration. Intimacy, cohesiveness, belonging, positive risk-taking, hope and competence were all deepened, given greater dimension, through humour (Brandler & Roman, 1999; Malekoff, 1997). During this trip, girls shared ideas about their future plans and careers; they began to inhabit the identity, if sometimes tentatively, of the professions they had chosen, making some of the following comments: 'When I become an actor I'm moving to New York City,' 'As a lawyer I want to make sure women are safe,' 'I'm going to start my own fashion design business,' and so on. It was a delight to see the girls having an expanded sense of self as potentially active agents in the public sphere.

The final session centred on participants putting together photo albums. For each trip I had brought my camera and two rolls of film. Members were told they could have anything of their choice photographed along the trip, and, if so inclined, they could use the camera and take their own photographs. Each member was given a photo album and decorative, thematically relevant stickers. Several copies of photographs were made from each outing, so that every member had a complete set from all the trips. The photo albums became photo journals that visually documented the life, vitality and range of the IHD group, and the power, potentiality and excellence of each participant. We had an enjoyable time assembling our albums, reminiscing and laughing throughout.

Results

The IHD girls' group was run as a pilot project on the reserve. No quantitative data was gathered. In preliminary discussions with the NCW director, we agreed that the group was to be about the girls, for the girls, without any pre- and post-test measures. Nothing was to be asked of the girls beyond their participation in the group, regular attendance, and willingness to explore their interests. Qualitative data was gathered informally, largely in the form of volunteered feedback, including member self-reports and anecdotal data from parents (Malekoff, 1997). Judging by this data the group was a success. All group members were enthusiastic about their new or strengthened career goals, all expressed excitement about the trips, and all disclosed regret that the ten sessions had come too quickly to an end. Throughout the project, girls developed more confidence, asking professors and students questions with greater ease during our field trips. As they investigated their interests, entertained the possibility of a meaningful and rewarding professional future, and entered into group discussions about their abilities and options, the girls became more critical of the scripted, circumscribed female role promulgated by media and the dominant culture. Members talked about the need to study hard to get into their preferred programs and their determination to attain their career goals. Some participants spoke of returning to the reserve to benefit the community with their professional skills, while others expressed a wish to live in a fast-paced and challenging big city. Underpinning both positions was a tone of empowerment and a sense that these girls had glimpsed a very real and bright possible future. In fact, several of the girls expressed that the IHD group gave them their first opportunity to experience a life beyond high school that seemed tangible and within reach.

Along with the girls' positive comments and observations, I received favourable feedback from all the parents. One parent told me that since her daughter's Dream Day, she was watching significantly less television and spending more time studying. This girl explained her behavioural change to her mother saying, 'If I am going to get into that university program, I have to start focusing more on my school work.' The mother was pleased to see her daughter's focus and initiative. This same mother also asked that I consider extending the IHD group, and just meet locally for weekly two- or three-hour sessions, as her daughter was benefiting greatly from the positive social interactions and the esteem-building empowerment approach. Another mother telephoned to say that the IHD group was having a 'very significant positive impact' on her daughter's life. She too asked if the group could be extended beyond the deadline. Other parents contacted me to say that their daughters were really enjoying the group, and one parent indicated the IHD was the highlight of his daughter's week. Two parents shared that their daughters, who often returned home from group activities feeling troubled and needing to process upsetting events, returned home from the IHD talkative, animated, wanting to share how their day unfolded. For a group that was designed to empower girls and to help them keep and express their voice, this feedback seemed to indicate that these goals were achieved.

Together with these positive indicators from daughters and parents alike, was the affirmative response of the community itself. Professionals, employees, and community members came to see the IHD group as a healthy community force. In informal discussions there was mention of supporting more programming of this kind. Some even considered using the IHD model as a prototype for groups with other at-risk sub-populations, adopting the same structure but modifying or substituting the organizing theme. All the qualitative data collected through members' comments, parents' feedback, and observations suggest that the IHD group has had a salutary impact on participating girls and the community.

Discussion

The first implementation of the IHD program clearly produced positive results. The group offered the girls several new opportunities, including the chance to be masters of their own destiny within the group context. That is, each girl was encouraged to conduct research, select a professional area, and decide exactly which program she wanted to visit on her Dream Day. This process in itself was greatly empowering as group members felt personal efficacy in experiencing the outcome of their choices. Reflecting on this experience, one girl stated, 'It was amazing to pick what I want to do, and then go for the day and have my plan actually happen. This was the best day.' When what is imposed upon most girls and women is the ideal of 'self-sacrifice,' the 'radically unrewarding handing over of their identity and energy to individual males ... and to ghostly institutional masters' (Daly, 1978, p. 374), the experience of authoring one's own destiny for a day, and a realization that one can create such possibilities for oneself in the future, is empowering and memorable. Like Ouspensky's (1982) description of a portal, providing an enlarged perspective of reality, the IHD project allowed members to understand that what seemed overwhelming was large, but manageable; what appeared out of reach was genuinely within their grasp; and what looked ineluctable was actually negotiable. Through the process of journeying, both inwardly and outwardly, the girls came to exhibit more confidence, more self-knowledge, and more interest in their needs, their lives and their future. Moreover the mutuality and peer support enabled the girls to begin to understand and combat the oppressive forces of misogynistic dominant culture messages. The most concise example of this was a few girls insisting that a popular radio song, that they used to enjoy, be turned off because the lyrics were demeaning to women.

Historically, one of the most effective methods of change is non-violent resistance (Junor, 1995; Gandhi, 1969; Martin Luther King, Jr., 2001). The consciousness-raising subtext of this group, not only around gender but also race and class, encouraged critique of and resistance to toxic messages from the dominant culture. In this manner, the model is consistent with social work values, promoting self-determination while simultaneously fostering larger social change. The impact of meeting and interacting with First Nations adults in the girls' chosen fields, cannot be underscored enough. On every trip we met with incredibly talented First Nations professionals and students, and without fail they all imparted the same motivational message: the girls could one day be in their shoes if they so desired. Lastly, it warrants reiteration, that a great deal of fun was had on our several road trips. The girls explored new terrain and extended boundaries in a positive way through the use of humour.

This model was developed as a result of learning that a number of girls on the reserve did not have future plans and dreams. When I entered into discussion with each of these girls to understand their experience, I learned that they simply did not think of themselves in the future. This concerned me, because without a larger vision or purpose to guide oneself, especially young adolescent girls growing up in a girl-poisoning culture, there is the hazard of being irretrievably lost. The dreams of our authentic self are what keep us directed on our self-determinative course. As Black Elk states, 'Sometimes dreams are wiser than waking' (1995, p. 10).

References

Abels, P. and Abels, S. (2002). Narrative social work with groups: Just in time. In S. Henry, J. East, and C. Schmitz (Eds.), *Social work with groups: Mining the gold.* New York: The Haworth Press

American Association of University Women. (1992). *How schools shortchange girls: The AAUW report.* New York: Marlow & Co

Azzarto, J. (1997). A young women's support group: Prevention of a different kind. *Health and Social Work, 22*(4), 299-306

Berman-Rossi, T. (2002). My love affair with stages of group development.

Social Work with Groups. 25(1/2), 151-158

Black Elk (1995). *Black Elk speaks: Being the life story of a holy man of the Oglala Sioux. As told through John G. Neihardt.* Lincoln: University of Nebraska Press

Bowling, S., Zimmerman, T., Carlson Daniels, K. (2000). 'Empower': A feminist consciousness-raising curriculum for adolescent women. *Journal of Child and Adolescent Group Therapy, 10*(1), 3-28

Brandler, S. and Roman, C. (1999). *Group work: Skills and strategies for effective interventions, 2ⁿᵈ edition.* New York: The Haworth Press

Canada. Royal Commission on Aboriginal Peoples. (1996). *Report of the Royal Commission on Aboriginal Peoples.* Volume 1. Ottawa: The Commission

Cox, E.O. (1991). The critical role of social action in empowerment oriented groups. *Social Work with Groups, 14*(3/4), 77-90

Daly, M. (1978). *Gyn-Ecology: The metaethics of radical feminism.* Boston: Beacon Press

de Beauvoir, S. (1953). *The second sex.* New York: Knopf

Dorney, J.A. (1995). Educating toward resistance: A task for women teaching girls. *Youth & Society, 27*(1), 55-72

Durst, D. (1992). The road to poverty is paid with good intentions: Social interventions and Indigenous Peoples. *International Social Work, 35,* 190-202

Erikson, E. (1968). *Identity, Youth and Crisis.* New York: Norton Publishers

Frideres, J.S. (1996). The Royal Commission on Aboriginal Peoples: The route to self-government? *The Canadian Journal of Native Studies,16*(2), 247-266

Gandhi, M. (1969). *Non-violent Resistance (Satyagraha).* New York: Schocken Books

Garland, J.A., Jones, H.E., and Kolodny, R.L. (1965). A model for stages of development in social work groups. In S. Bernstein (Ed.), *Explorations in Group Work.* (pp. 17-71). Boston: Boston University School of Social Work

Gerbner, G., Gross, L., Morgan, M., and Signorielli, N. (1993). Growing up with television: The cultivation perspective. In J. Bryant and D. Zillman (Eds.), *Media effects: Advances in theory and research.* Hillsdale, NJ: Lawrence Erlbaum

Gilligan, C., Rogers, A.G., & Tolman, D.L. (Eds.). (1991). *Women, girls and psychotherapy: Reframing resistance.* Binghampton, NY: Haworth

Heilman, E. (1998). The struggle for self: Power and identity in adolescent girls. *Youth & Society, 30*(2), 182-208

hooks, b. (2000). *Feminism is for everybody: Passionate politics.* Cambridge, MA: South End Press

Junor, B. (1995). *Greenham Common women's peace camp: A history of non-*

violent resistance, 1984-1995. London: Working Press

Kilbourne, J. (1990). Beauty ... and the beast of advertising. *Media & Values,* 49

Kilbourne, J. (2003). The more you subtract the more you add: Cutting girls down to size. In G. Dines and J. Humez (Eds.), *Gender, race, and class in media: A text reader.* Thousand Oaks, CA: Sage Publications

LaForme, H.S. (1991). Indian Sovereignty : What does it mean ? *The Canadian Journal of Native Studies, 11*(2), 253-266

LaRocque, E. (1996). The colonization of a Native woman scholar. In Christine Miller and Patricia Chuchryk (Eds.), *Women of the First Nations: Power, wisdom, and strength*

Luther King, Jr., M. (2001). *A call to conscience: The landmark speeches of Dr. Martin Luther King, Jr.* New York: Warner Books

Malekoff, A. (1997). *Group work with adolescents.* New York: Guilford Press

Mander, J. (1991). *In the absence of the sacred: The failure of technology and the survival of the Indian Nations.* San Francisco: Sierra Club Books

McKenzie, B., Seidl, E., and Bone, N. (1995). Child and family service standards in First Nations: An action research project. *Child Welfare, 74*(3), 633-653

Middleman, R. and Wood, G.G. (1990). From social group work to social work with groups. *Social Work with Groups.* 13(3), 3-20

Miller, J.R. (1996). *Shingwauk's vision: A history of Native residential schools.* Toronto: Toronto University Press

Northern, H. and Kurland, R. (2001). *Social work with groups, 3rd edition.* New York: Columbia University Press

Ouspensky, P.D. (1982). *Tertium Organum: The third canon of thought, a key to the enigmas of the world.* New York: Vintage Books

Pipher, M. (1994). *Reviving Ophelia: Saving the selves of adolescent girls.* New York: Ballantine Books

Rose, S. (1998). *Group work with children and adolescents: Prevention and intervention in school and community systems.* Thousand Oaks: Sage Publications

Saulnier, C.F. (2000). Incorporating feminist theory into social work practice: Group work examples. *Social Work with Groups, 23*(1), 5-29

Schiller, L.Y. (1997). Rethinking stages of development in women's groups: Implications for practice. *Social Work with Groups, 20*(3)

Schiller, L.Y. (2003). Women's group development from a relational model and a new look at facilitator influence on group development. In M.B. Cohen and A. Mullender (Eds.), *Gender and Groupwork,* (pp. 16-31). New York: Routledge

Signorielli, N. and Morgan, M. (1990). (Eds.). *Cultivation analysis: New directions in media effects research.* Newbury Park, CA: Sage

Spira, M., Grossman, S., and Wolff-Bensdorf, J. (2002). Voice and identity in a bicultural/bilingual environment. *Child and Adolescent Social Work Journal, 19*(2), 115-138

Steinberg, D.M. (2004). *The Mutual Aid Approach to Working with Groups: Helping People Help One Another, 2ed.* Binghamton, NY: The Haworth Press

Stone, M. (1998). Journaling with clients. *Journal of Individual Psychology. Special Issue: Narrative therapy and Adlerian psychology, 54*(4), 535-545. Winnipeg: University of Manitoba Press

Walsh-Burke, K., and Scanlone, P. (2000). Beyond reviving Ophelia: Groups for girls 12-14 and women who care about them. *Social Work with Groups, 23*(1), 71-81

Wood, P. and Clay, C. (1996). Perceived structural barriers and academic performance among American Indian high school students. *Youth & Society, 28*(1), 40-61

4
Using literature groups to teach diversity

Mari Ann Graham

I have been using literature groups (otherwise known as reading groups or book groups) to teach diversity for a number of years. Novels and memoirs can help students appreciate the struggles of immigrants adapting to western culture (Fadiman, 1995), become more personally aware of their whiteness and privilege (Lazarre, 1997), get inside the complexities of transgender identity (Feinberg, 1993), and develop empathy for dwarfs and comprehend the many ways that people get caught in systemic oppression (Hegi, 1994). Using literature has been an engaging way to teach the *realities of diversity*, as opposed to merely talking intellectually *about* it. Experiences with these reading groups are among my most rewarding moments in the classroom. I would like to begin by first articulating a rationale for using *literature* (as opposed to conventional texts), moving to a rationale for using literature *groups*. This will be followed by a brief description of structure and format that I have used for these groups, and a few general recommendations for those who want to use groups of this nature. I will conclude with what I have learned from using these groups via actual experiences of students, noting both the rewards and challenges of using this method of instruction.

Why use literature?

OK, I confess – I can't stand textbooks. I know I'm not supposed to say that, but it's true. I'm an educator and I can hardly bear the thought of textbooks each year. Well, that's a little dramatic, I suppose. The truth is, I don't find them particularly engaging. In short, they bore me. And I figure if I'm bored, this doesn't bode well for my students. I think my lack of engagement has to do with the predictability and sterile way in which information is presented. Everything is so orderly – each main point, followed by relevant sub points (A, B and C), with an occasional example tossed in for application or special emphasis. And to the extent that we need to present information in orderly, sequenced ways, textbooks are, of course, the most efficient way to get the job done. But since I am less and less inclined to teach from the traditional paradigm in which it is assumed that teachers have information which can readily be transmitted to students, and since the older I get I am less and less inclined toward efficiency (at least in terms of how it is typically conceived), I find myself tolerating academia's dependence on textbooks, while actively searching for more authentic ways of engaging students (as well as myself) in the learning process.

Use of literature – novels, short stories, poetry – is one such way. Literature, like music or the daily news, is much more like real life. It is full of surprises. It reflects a particular point of view, and requires that the reader temporarily suspend his or her reality in order to enter the frame of the writer. Often, the act of suspending one's own point of view is instructive in and of itself. What we learn about *ourselves* (where our assumptions are, where it is most difficult to 'let go,' where our particular resistances are) can be every bit as important as *what* we are trying to learn. While one might argue correctly that this temporary suspension of one's frame of reference is necessary when reading anything, when reading literature, the point of view of the author is not so readily taken for granted. Writers have the responsibility of actively engaging their readers in their point of view and can't assume that readers will passively receive the so called 'factual' information presumed to be 'true' by textbook authors. Because of this difference, readers of literature are forced to use their imagination and themselves in important ways.

But this more active posture on the part of the reader (and all that goes with it) isn't the only reason for using literature. Literature gets the reader 'inside' other people's stories, in contrast to textbooks, which keep readers at an analytical distance. Good literature makes us feel as well as think, and somehow changes us as a result of the experience. Literature, like other art forms, offers opportunities for vicarious learning that more closely approximates real life. If effective, literature has a way of getting in 'under the radar' of our habitual defenses, engaging even our unconscious selves, and leading us into places we would otherwise never go. That's the power of any art form – to take us *there*. Textbooks by their very nature simply cannot take us *there*.

Since diversity content is infinite, and since the goal in social work education is not the mere transmission of sterile information but rather the development of genuine appreciation for diversity and increased self-awareness of personal bias, using literature (and other art forms) makes good sense. A story can deal simultaneously with many forms of diversity and with multi-layered responses in ways that a textbook cannot. Stories don't so much *tell* as they *evoke*. And I would argue that diversity education that is not evocative is not only useless, it is potentially dangerous. Dangerous because telling students *about* discrimination without helping them see how we are all victims and perpetrators can reinforce the all too common tendency to blame and respond punitively, rather than encouraging them to do the hard work of sorting through the complexities inherent in most diversity issues. Dangerous because setting up unrealistic expectations that lead to professional guilt and/or burnout damages professionals and clients in ways that we still find difficult to articulate. Dangerous because information without transformation is like an accident waiting to happen.

Ironically, however, we use textbooks because they seem 'safer.' They don't evoke much in the moment, and therefore, the implicit dangers are obscured. Evocative teaching methods seem more dangerous because instructors lose a measure of control. Once students are evoked by literature, the instructor has to be willing to follow wherever that might lead. This can be unsettling for teachers who have been conditioned to maintain control as an indicator of their competence. But some loss of control is inherent in the shift toward a more critical, constructivist pedagogy.

Consistent with the movement towards critical/constructivist pedagogy in social work education (Graham, 2003; Graham, 2002; Laird, 1993; Weick, 1993; Jackson & Taylor, 1991; Brigham, 1977), use of literature in the classroom can bring out students' 'lived experience' of diversity, assist them in de-constructing and re-constructing their assumptions and facilitate a genuine appreciation of the ways that perceptions are tied to experiences. Instead of talking 'about' diversity (from a distance), literature brings diversity 'up close and personal.' Literature provides an arena for students to personally experience themselves as 'the other' as well as experiencing others' otherness.

Besides, reading literature is much more enjoyable. Students and faculty alike bemoan not having the time to read the things they would really like to read because they have to do assigned [textbook] readings, write (or grade) papers, and other 'academic' activities that are considered more legitimate, but less fun. Reading for 'fun' has almost become an oxymoron for students. The use of reading groups can encourage and develop the love of reading and lifelong learning. Reading works of literature and taking class time to discuss them (in anything other than literature courses), however, seems to be a luxury that our crowded, professional curricula can't afford. Using literature (as well as other art forms) is likened to classroom entertainment and appears to transgress the implicit mandate for seriousness and rigor in higher education. What this really implies is that serious, rigorous study can't also be fun. But there are those who celebrate a kind of teaching that enables 'movement against and beyond boundaries' because of how it makes 'education the practice of freedom' (hooks, 1994). This transgression alone may be exciting enough for some; for social work educators, there is even more cause for excitement.

Why literature groups?

The popularity of reading groups in general is also well documented in the literature. There are lots of reasons for this popularity. Perhaps the most obvious reason for reading literature in groups is that it is important to be able to talk about what one has read with others who have read the same thing. To be able to talk about what one has read extends the vicarious nature of the learning beyond one's own interpretations and deconstructions. It is both challenging and fun. Challenging because direct experience with other points of view exposes limitations and inherent biases in one's own perspective. Fun, because such exposure, while certainly uncomfortable at times, is also quite liberating. On a very basic level, it is fun to discover what we don't know in the context of what we do know in the company of peers, friends, and people we trust.

In social work education, teaching group process skills is an integral part of the curriculum. Student groups can be used not only as a supplemental method for elaborating and integrating course content, they can also become the subject of learning itself. In other words, small groups, if used deliberately and with some supervision, can become an arena for dis-covering curricular content and for co-creating knowledge. If students and faculty attend to the group's process (as well as to specified group outcomes), reading groups create opportunities for increasing student awareness and skill related to group process, group dynamics, roles they assume as members and as facilitators, while simultaneously providing a forum in which students can bring what they already know to the table and have an active role in shaping curricular content. Rather than passively receiving information, their 'lived experience' of the subject becomes part of a dynamic process of knowledge creation. This is obviously a lot more interesting and 'fun' for both teachers and students. In short, it is exhilarating. It is what makes teaching and learning worth every bit of effort we put into it.

Use of literature groups is also a relevant teaching strategy in social work education because of how literature group dynamics parallel several narrative practice principles. These groups provide opportunities for 'externalizing conversations,' which are all about creating distance between people and their problems so that they do not identify so fully with their problems and thereby become immobilized by 'problem-saturated perceptions' (White, 2002). The extent to which practitioners, for example, have become immobilized by the problem of their lack of cultural competence is significant. Discussing literature does allow students some distance from the subject, so that they don't become 'swallowed up' by a problem that often feels overwhelming and produces high levels of anxiety. Like clients, students need to be able to have 'the conversation' without it feeling like a personal indictment of who they are. Then, they are free to explore problems more fully, with less defensiveness so that they can have 're-authoring conversations' (White, 2002). In narrative practice, these conversations provide opportunities to experience oneself apart from the dominant story line so that one can change patterns of behavior. This, too, is of critical importance for students who not only need to become aware of their biases and insensitivities, but who also need to develop strategies for dealing with them. Reading groups are a wonderful context for beginning these 're-authoring conversations.' When students share what they have learned in their reading groups with the entire class, these 're-authoring conversations' are expanded to include others outside their group.

Since social work educators are mandated to teach diversity content and content related to group work, use of literature groups in the classroom can be a lively way of fulfilling both purposes.

Description of format

Background

In a required foundation level practice course, we have historically included a unit on unintentional discrimination. We used a required text on unintentional racism to identify the dynamics of unintentional racism (Ridley, 1995), extrapolating this content to make application to other forms of unintended discrimination and to begin some dialogue about what social work practitioners can do to minimize unintentional discrimination and more effectively deal with it when it arises. The text, while provocative in many respects and certainly an adequate starting point for this unit, either seemed to go over the heads of students, or else shut many of them down. Conversations on this topic were (and still are) highly sensitized. It was my observation that the text kept conversations at an academic level of abstraction, and was, therefore, too remote and distant from student experience. I tried various ways of making the content more concrete and accessible (with mixed success) and then one year decided to offer several reading options for that unit. In addition to the textbook, I gave students several other options – *Stonebutch Blues* (Feinberg, 1993), *Beyond the Whiteness of Whiteness* (Lazarre, 1997), and *The Spirit Catches You and You Fall Down* (Fadiman, 1997).

Students were required to select one of these, read it, and work in a small group to present what they learned to the whole class. Facilitation of the group was rotated among group members. Interestingly, the textbook drew nearly as much student interest as the others (I gave brief reviews of each book prior to students making their selections, attempting to 'pitch' each as optimistically as I could), and we had four student groups of roughly the same size. Each group agreed to present to the class for roughly an hour and a half. The focus of the presentation was on identifying the dynamics of unintended discrimination (How does it work? How does it happen?) and how social workers can best respond. I encouraged students to be creative and involve the class actively in whatever they do (as opposed to giving a report). The students then (and now) never ceased to amaze me in terms of the creative ways they find to engage their classmates. These class sessions were and are some of the liveliest and most memorable.

Evolution of the format

Since that first year a few things have changed. The presentations have become longer – two to two and a half hours instead of one to one and a half hours. While students are initially intimidated by the length of time suggested, we quickly find that when we really engage the whole class (rather than lecture), the time goes by quickly. Even with the additional time allotted to these presentations, it is often the case that we wish we had even more time to devote to these issues. Students really do want (and need) to process these issues when given a safe format in which to do it.

The original text is still made available as an optional text but after student interest in it declined, I included another option, *Stones From the River* (Hegi, 1994), and students now select from among these four. Almost any work of fiction (or nonfiction) that deals with an issue of diversity can be used. I tend to select nonfiction that is *not* 'textbooky' for the reasons I've already named. Often, students can't wait to read these. Faculty may even select and rotate books that students really want to read (but say they don't have time to read).

This unit on unintentional discrimination happens to be taught during the same time in the semester as a unit on group work. One year when negotiating assignment options with students, they suggested the creation of reading groups as an in-class activity for the group work unit using the text they selected for the unintentional discrimination unit. Many of them had heard about or participated in reading groups and so long as they had to read the books anyway, they asked why not create and use those groups to learn about group work? Their interest was the ever creative effort to 'kill two birds with one stone,' and I admit having been intrigued by the idea. An avid participant in a monthly reading group myself, it never occurred to me to suggest this as an option for *them*! The results of this shift in format have been positive. In contrast to other in-class group activities (fishbowls, role playing of groups, etc.) students appreciate the fact that these are *real* groups, formed on the basis of a common interest in a book. I observed that they did become *real* groups in terms of cohesion and other group dynamics. They appreciate having some class time (I typically allowed 40-45 minutes, once a week for 6 weeks) to discuss their experience of the book with their peers.

The fact that students are required to give a presentation to the entire class at the end of the 6 week period might suggest to some that it is a task group. In fact, it can become a task group quite easily since it is generally less threatening to focus on planning a presentation, than to share personal reactions to readings. But I encourage students to see the group and facilitate it primarily as an educational/support group. I encourage them to see their growth and development as professionals as primary, the task of presenting to the class as secondary. Prior to beginning these in-class group sessions, we cover some foundation group work content (stages of group, group dynamics, leadership issues, planning a group, and beginning a group), and once groups have begun meeting, we continue our review of group work content in the classroom (assessment in groups, treatment group methods, task group methods, evaluating and terminating groups) for the next several weeks. Students seem to 'get' the group work content and experience its immediacy as a result of having this concurrent group experience. There is some predictable anxiety when it is their turn to lead the group, and in dealing with some of the issues that come up in the group. This appears to keep students focused and interested in the group work content discussed in class. Students are still meeting in their in-class reading groups when we shift the classroom focus to another unit of study, and this has not been at all problematic. After groups have ended, students write a group work self-assessment, assessing their roles as member and as leader (drawing on other experiences they have had in groups), identifying their personal strengths and challenges, and discussing what they have learned about group dynamics and process.

I have gravitated to having the group presentations during the last few class sessions because they are often high energy (at a time when all of us need the energy), and also because this also gives students additional time (if they need it) to plan their presentations to the class.

Recommendations

Having used this method now for a number of years, I am confident in recommending its use to any instructor teaching diversity content, as well as to social work educators teaching practice, policy, field or human behavior courses. It can be easily adapted to meet course objectives, but certain things are worth noting, as follows:

- *Allow students some choice in the selection process.*
  I have tended to present students with a menu of options (often based on recommendations/feedback from former students). In this way, they become invested in the process by virtue of their choice and have a common starting point for dialogue with other students who also selected that book. To keep this manageable, instructors will need to limit the number of options, so that their are adequate numbers of students in each group. I have found that groups work well with 5 to 7 students.

- *Use books that are interesting to you and that you suspect will be interesting to your students.*
  Your interest and enthusiasm is an important ingredient in the process, every bit as important as student engagement. Rather than select books that you think social workers *should* read, select books that they (and you) really *want* to read.

- *Provide consultation/supervision to groups.*
  I have found this to be essential in terms of being able to provide assistance to students when they encounter challenging group dynamics and to help them more thoroughly integrate the readings. I recommend having an 'unobtrusive' presence by occasionally sitting in on groups and/or being available for consultation with groups during the times they are meeting. It is also important to the overall success of the model that the instructor stay connected to what is happening in the groups. Dynamics in the large group (class as a whole) may play out in groups and vice versa. Since discussions are often personal and may be emotionally charged, having the instructor present/available contributes to a sense of safety.

- *Allow in-class time for groups.*
  This communicates the importance of the activity, i.e., that it is just as important as instructor's lecture or any other class activity. Allowing class time for groups also minimizes logistical challenges that arise if students are required to meet outside of class for all meetings.

- *Combine the use of these groups with introspective writing.*
  I encourage students to journal about their experiences in their reading group, so that they have plenty of raw material to reflect

upon when writing up their group work self-assessment and also to facilitate dialogue in their groups. If a written self-assessment is not required, I would see this kind of reflective writing as even more critical.

Two illustrations

There are many illustrations I could give to illustrate the quality of student engagement and learning in these groups. But two stand out as examples of what can happen in the process, how supervision is important and how students benefit from these kinds of group experiences.

One of the most dramatic experiences occurred when a student, let's call her Julie, was purchasing Leslie Feinberg's, Stonebutch Blues at a local Barnes and Noble bookstore. The year I decided to shift to this format, students were given ample time to order the book of their choice from a local bookstore and begin reading by a certain date. This was no problem since the books were all in print and readily available for purchase. It also simplified book orders (since I had no way of knowing in advance how many student copies of each to order from our book store). When Julie asked about the book, she was directed to the Gay/Lesbian Studies section, and a clerk made a comment to her along the lines of, 'So this is what lesbians look like nowadays.' Julie, not a lesbian, was immediately offended at the remark and told the clerk she was not a lesbian, but was getting the book for a class. Her husband who was browsing nearby came over to see what the problem was. The clerk apologized to Julie and her husband, and the event might have been relatively uneventful had Julie not decided to share the experience in the context of her reading group.

When she shared the experience in the group, she talked about how she was first of all angered at the presumption that she was a lesbian just because she was purchasing the book. This led to some discussion in her small group (and later to discussion with the whole class) about how it feels to have your sexual orientation incorrectly taken for granted – ironically, the experience that lesbians often have in reverse. And this 'ah-ha,' big as it was for this student, was just the beginning. She remembered, and reported to the group, feeling embarrassed, as though everybody was looking at her, and was somewhat 'paranoid,' wondering what they were thinking after the clerk made the comment. This, too, she used to develop an empathic point of reference for understanding the challenges that lesbians and transgender people face in homophobic settings. Finally, and this was the real clincher, she also reported feeling guilty that she felt embarrassed. Her rational mind said, why should I be embarrassed because somebody thought I was a lesbian? I don't think there's anything wrong with being a lesbian. But if I really thought there wasn't anything wrong with being a lesbian, why did I feel guilt and shame? This, of course, led to some very important dialogue around the nature of internalized oppression, and how we are often unaware of the extent to which we have internalized certain values until we have experiences like this that effectively remove our blinders. The whole class was then able to talk about the various blind spots that social workers have and what we are able to do about them. And all of this, from a brief encounter while purchasing a book!

Another, quite vivid experience occurred rather recently when two students who decided to read *Beyond the Whiteness of Whiteness* (Lazarre, 1997) experienced a conflict that 'hooked' the other members of their group in important ways, and became grist for the mill for the rest of the class. Rhonda, a white student, welcomed the opportunity to read the book and hoped it would shed some light on difficulties she had relating to a black female student in our MSW program, having had virtually no contact with blacks prior to beginning the program. She admitted not having thought very much about what it meant to be white all of her life, and very much wanted concrete 'answers' from the book about how to deal with black people. This motivation resulted in her taking experiences from the book and generalizing them to other groups (to white women, for example) in her sincere effort to try and relate to what the author (a white mother of black sons) was talking about. A black female in her group, Shaniqua, took issue with this approach, and articulated her anger that such comparisons 'water down' and undermine the reality of racism against blacks in this country, and was clearly not the intention of the author.

The dialogue in the reading group quickly polarized (as discussions of race often do), and members of the group felt pressured to take sides with either Rhonda or Shaniqua. Since the others (all white females) were social work students, however, this was tricky. Everybody said they could understand Shaniqua's point. They also could see Rhonda's intention. They consulted with me and asked me to sit in on their next group session and help mediate what they saw as a difficult problem.

When I did so, I observed what I just detailed, reflected back to them what I saw, and asked them to consider how their attachment to a 'position' was getting in the way of seeing what was at stake for the other side (a direct reference to another text used in the course, Fisher & Ury's *Getting to Yes*). At this point Shaniqua said that she can appreciate how Rhonda and other white people try to understand the black experience by using their own experiences, but that the comparisons just don't cut it. Rhonda then said something like, 'wow, it must really be frustrating for you to have people like me doing what I just did. I never realized that before now.' The irony, of course, is that Shaniqua's insistence that whites could not 'cross over' in the way Rhonda was attempting to (a point discussed at some length in Lazarre's work) along with Rhonda's persistence, ultimately did result in a 'crossing over.'

Conclusions

In the first scenario, the student scarcely thought the event worth reporting to her group until I (after overhearing her report her incredulity at the arrogance of the clerk to a friend) suggested that there might be value in processing this experience with her group. She subsequently reported to the entire class that this may have been one of her most memorable experiences as a graduate student. And while the second scenario clearly reflects group member awareness of the need for outside consultation because of the discomfort experienced by group members, what both cases reveal is the critical importance of supervision of these groups. This need is not so much one of ensuring that students stay on task or other accountability functions, but in terms of providing students with useful frames within which they can process their own experiences, learn from them and empower themselves and others. I shudder to think of what might have been lost to the individual students involved, to the two student groups, to both classes as a whole, and subsequent groups of students who have only heard about these experiences had these students not been encouraged to process their experiences. And in many ways, these two experiences are not all that unusual or exceptional. What is perhaps unusual and exceptional is having the courage and taking the time to process experiences like this. These are the 'teachable moments' that are almost always there, waiting below the surface for the courageous and caring eye to notice.

These 'teachable moments' are just as scary for teachers as they are for students, which may help us see why using textbooks and other less evocative teaching methods are often preferred. We don't know ahead of time where these experiences will take us or our students. But then, isn't that the whole point of education? The question isn't so much a 'how to' question, how do we engage them, keep their interest, etc., but rather, do *we* have the guts? And, if we have the guts to use literature and other art forms to evoke authentic engagement from students, we need to have the guts to follow the process with them, using all of who we are to help them be all of who they are. This is one of the most important things I have learned over the years. I need to 'show up' for the process if I have any hope that students will. They need to be able to see me go willingly into the darkness, and maybe then, they can trust that they, too, will come out alive.

I've also learned that students are much more resilient than we think. They don't break, and neither will we, which of course leads to a basic tenant of empowering education – transformation is usually painful. Pain and discomfort are part of the process of change. Aversion to the discomfort and avoidance of that which is potentially painful robs students (as well as clients) of empowering opportunities for growth. But once again, the teacher (or therapist) must be willing to go there. The challenges of going there for teachers have to do with dealing with loss of control and the willingness to experience our own discomfort as well as that of students. That discomfort notwithstanding, teaching diversity in this way is ever-fresh, invigorating, and keeps us on our toes. It is worth every bit of the effort involved, and ultimately much more rewarding than conventional content-driven approaches.

References

Brigham, T. (1977). Liberation in social work education: Applications from Paulo Freire. *Journal of Education for Social Work, 13(3)*, 5-11

Feinberg, L. (1993). *Stonebutch blues.* Ithaca, NY: Firebrand Books

Hegi, U. (1994). *Stones from the river.* NY: Simon & Schuster

hooks, b. (1994). *Teaching to transgress: Education as the practice of freedom.*

NY: Routledge

Jackson, S. & Taylor, I. (1991). Enquiry and action learning: Modeling community practice in social work education. Paper presented at conference on social work education, March

Laird, J. (Ed.) (1993). *Revisioning social work education: A social constructivist approach.* Binghampton, NY: Haworth

Lazarre, J. (1997). *Beyond the whiteness of whiteness.* Durham, NC: Duke University Press

Ridley, C. (1995). *Overcoming unintentional racism in counseling and therapy.* Thousand Oaks, CA: Sage

Weick, A. (1993). Reconstructing social work education, *Journal of teaching in social work, 8(1/2)*, 11-30

Weick, A. (1997). Personal communication with the author, November 26

White, M. (2002)

5
The use of 'twelve-step' concepts of recovery in group work with mentally retarded and developmentally disabled adults

Juli Kempner

Introduction

It has only been recently recognized, within the past twenty years, that substance abuse is a specific problem in the population of mentally retarded and developmentally disabled (MRDD) adults. Although some suggestions have been made in the literature about treatment techniques, it has yet to be established what are the most useful methods for working with MRDD individuals who have been diagnosed with substance abuse problems. However, it has been documented that for the general population, there is a strong positive relationship between participation in twelve-step programs and long-term sobriety. Support for attendance at twelve-step programs and the use of twelve-step concepts in group work are useful in sobriety treatment with the MRDD population, and both can be incorporated into agency work.

There are very few agencies in the country that provide sobriety services for mentally retarded and developmentally disabled adults, and even fewer that follow a twelve-step model and encourage participation in twelve-step programs. Many agencies underutilize twelve-step programs because they are seen as unprofessional. Another perceived, although unverified obstacle, is that twelve-step programs require a certain cognitive skill level that MRDD adults do not possess.

Literature review

Prior to the 1980s, very little empirical or systematic research had been done on substance abuse in the MRDD population. Most of the early theories were a combination of anecdotal stories and suppositions. This situation changed dramatically when many individuals were released into the community after years of institutionalization. When this happened, they became vulnerable to a society in which substance abuse has become an ever-increasing problem. Once substance abuse was identified as an issue, there were initial attempts to assess the extent of the problem, but no consensus was reached on whether there was more or less substance abuse in the MRDD community than in the general population. Research then shifted to focusing on treatment, with a general agreement that specialized treatment was necessary.

Early research

Developmental Disability Disorders is a large category of disorders defined by the Diagnostic and Statistical Manual of Mental Disorders (DSM IV-TR), as being characterized by a predominant disruption in the acquisition of cognitive, language, motor, or social skills. It may involve a general delay, as in Mental Retardation; or a delay or failure to progress, as in Specific and Pervasive Disability Disorders. Mental Retardation is defined by a standard Intelligence Quotient test score below 70, plus deficits in two or more areas of life activity such as self-care, communication, home living, interpersonal skills, use of community resources, and self-direction, manifested before the age of eighteen years. (A.H.R.C. Resource Manual; American Psychiatric Association, 1994.)

Krischef and Dinitto (1981) did the first systematized investigation of the prevalence of alcoholism in the community by surveying both alcoholism treatment programs (ATP's) and associations for retarded individuals (ARI's) in several cities. The data suggested that similar to the general population, MRDD individuals with alcohol problems do not come into contact with treatment programs until the problem is severe, in fact, many come in with alcohol related arrests. While almost seventy percent of the ATP's felt that it might take significantly longer amounts of time to treat MRDD substance abusers, and used specialized techniques, more than half believed that the treatments were as successful. No one indicated a consistent belief that the MRDD clients were more susceptible to alcohol abuse than the general population.

Delouch and Greer (1981) found that MR individuals might have more preexisting health and medical problems, which are in turn exacerbated by substance abuse, making treatment more difficult. Krischef and Dinitto (1984) interviewed over 200 clients from 24 programs serving the mildly retarded in Florida and found data that suggested that drinking among mentally retarded (MR) adults is similar to that in the general population. Krischef (1986) also suggested that it might take longer to treat mentally retarded individuals.

Finally, Westermeyer, Phaobtong, and Neider (1988) conducted a landmark study, which set out to clarify the status of substance abuse in the mentally retarded population. The demographic characteristics, family and childhood history, substance abuse patterns, and substance related problems of 40 mildly retarded adults were compared with the same data for 40 non-MR substance abusers. The data suggested that both MR and general population substance abusers manifest similar pathological substance use patterns, as well as similar behavioral, psychological, and social problems, and both reflect the same prevalence of abuse. There is also a risk of adverse consequences with use of small quantities of drugs. Westermeyer, Kemp, and Nugent (1996) surveyed 348 adults in two university substance abuse facilities and found that six percent of the overall sample was MRDD, postulating that MRDD individuals may be at increased risk of drug abuse, with a higher rate of failure of treatment. They also confirmed that less substance abuse might result in more severe problems in a vulnerable MRDD individual, again, partially due to already limited social and cognitive skills.

Focus on treatment

An early study done by Smalls (1980/81) provided anecdotal data on this population concerning the use of group therapy labeled 'Emotions Anonymous'. Counselors ran weekly group therapy sessions in which they simplified the twelve steps of Alcoholics Anonymous (AA) into group exercises. Smalls (1980/81) suggested that social skills, relaxation, and problem solving are potential focus areas for treatment. Delaney and Poling (1990) reported on a specialized treatment program in Maine with three components: assessment, treatment, and aftercare, and emphasized short term reinforcement for appropriate behavior and encouraged involvement in Alcoholics Anonymous.

Obstacles to treatment include the fact that substance abuse is often seen as a secondary disability and is not a primary focus of treatment (Benshoff, 1990); substance abuse is unrecognized in medical settings (Shipley, Taylor & Falvo, 1990); and mentally retarded clients are not asked about substance abuse (Frieden, 1990). This is in spite of the fact that the treatment variables for substance abuse in the MRDD community are the same as in the general population. (Moore & Polsgrove, 1991). It is not unusual even today for social workers in the field to express surprise that substance abuse is a problem in the MRDD population.

Lottman (1994) suggested targeting subgroups at risk: persons with dual diagnosis of mental retardation and substance abuse; individuals who take psychotropic and/or neuroleptic medications, or have medical complications; and MR adolescents who are mainstreamed into normal schools. Paxon (1995) underscored the need for specific relapse prevention techniques for this population: presentation of information using simplified materials, and modified individual and group counseling.

Christian and Poling (1997) did a comprehensive review of the literature on drug abuse in this population, concluding only that no reliable and preferred practices for detection, treatment, or prevention of substance abuse have been empirically validated. Christian and Poling (1997) also discussed modification of AA materials, which included one to one oral review of the program materials, and use of video or pictorial renditions of the twelve steps to facilitate comprehension. Burgard, Donohue, Azrin and Teichner (2000) also concluded that cognitively impaired individuals may have a harder time just 'saying no to drugs', and have poor insight regarding negative consequences of substance abuse, necessitating more finely tuned treatment modalities.

Twelve-step programs as a treatment tool

Alcoholics Anonymous has long been identified as an important tool for long term sobriety. Thurstin, Alfano, and Sherer (1986) found that male veteran AA attendees reported better outcome than non-attendees, which suggests that long-term success correlates positively with AA participation. Subsequent researchers also concluded that AA involvement has been associated with many alcohol dependent individuals achieving long term sobriety. (Emrick, 1987; McBride, 1991). However, there is not total agreement in this area. Emrick, Tonigan, Montgomery and Little (1993), in a meta-analysis of previous studies, found that fifty-four percent of the studies found a positive relationship between AA attendance and sobriety, thirty-six percent of the studies found no relationship, and ten percent found a negative relationship. For the studies that did indicate a positive relationship, a common thread was that greater involvement in AA could predict lower alcohol consumption.

Other studies show that the level of involvement with the twelve-step program is important. Leech (1992) suggested that AA participants who have sponsors are less likely to relapse, while Montgomery, Miller, and Tonigan (1995) found that the extent of AA involvement was predictive of positive outcome: less alcohol consumption and better functioning in life. Connor, Tonigan and Miller (2001) found that AA participation is positively correlated to self-efficacy to prevent drinking and number of abstinent days after inpatient treatment.

Sobriety Services at the Association for the Help of Retarded Children

The Association for the Help of Retarded Children (AHRC) is an outpatient treatment facility in New York City, where this writer did a field internship as a group worker. AHRC provides group and individual therapy for MRDD adult clients using a twelve-step model of recovery.

Each client attends a minimum of two group sessions per week, with topics such as orientation to recovery; relapse and recovery, alcohol and drug education; the tools of recovery; relationships and feelings in recovery, and work readiness. Groups are structured on a continuum for those in the early stages of recovery, those with a year or more sobriety, referred to as 'clean time', and those with several years of sobriety. Graduates of the program stay connected through alumni groups. Within all of these groups, the twelve-steps concepts such as: 'one day at a time', asking for help, working with a sponsor (guide), going to meetings, sharing in meetings, doing service, and identifying with feelings of others in recovery, are explained, discussed, role played, and reinforced.

The twelve steps of recovery of the AA program are discussed and related to clients' experience. Definitions of key concepts are stressed – particularly the idea of being 'powerless' – not in one's life, but over the substance or the addiction itself, as members learn more about addiction as a disease. Member of AA come to the facility twice a week to provide on-site Alcoholics Anonymous meetings, which clients can attend voluntarily.

Some of the clients have achieved and maintained sobriety for over five years, and of those with long term sobriety – practically all attend AA meetings regularly, either at the facility or in the community. Discussion with them reveals that the process of getting comfortable in the meetings is the same as for non-MRDD participants – it is difficult in the beginning, but for the most part, other members are warm and welcoming. All felt that the AA meetings helped reinforce the work done at AHRC toward achieving and maintaining sobriety in individual and group sessions.

How the twelve steps of recovery work

Smith (1993) elaborated on the process of integration into the 12-step group and how that process builds self-esteem, comfort, and the ability to take risks, all of which promote the skills required for maintaining sobriety. Rappaport (1993) posits that it is through the telling of and listening to stories that members of AA transform their lives. The phenomenon that unfolds in a twelve-step meeting is equally available to MRDD individuals as people who can who can understand a story and identify with a fellow member's feelings.

Davis and Jansen (1998) reviewed the criticism of AA and offered a way of understanding AA as a place where identity transformation takes place through the use of metaphor and storytelling. They say that the single-minded nonpolitical focus of AA challenges Western cultural expectations regarding professionalism, power, and treatment models. AA is not treatment. It is something very different, and the inability to name and categorize exactly what it is appears troublesome to many professionals. The stumbling block for many professionals is the misconception that AA advocates powerlessness, but AA acknowledges powerlessness over alcohol *only*, not total powerlessness over one's life.

Narcotics Anonymous is also recognized as a useful treatment modality (Peyrot, 1985). The theory of drug abuse posed by NA is that it is the attributes of addiction that cause problems for addicts, not the particular substance. The key to recovery lies in the process through which the person is socially integrated into a group of others with similar issues. (Peyrot,1985). These concepts reflect the ideas of mutual aid used in the processes that group workers employ.

Reading, writing, and a certain level of cognition is not a requirement for twelve-step membership or abstinence. It is the shared human experience that produces the desired effect. This writer observed many MRDD individuals tell their story, listen to others people's stories, and identify, both in AA meetings and in regular group sessions at AHRC. That may be part of what begins the change in attitude that begins the shift to sobriety and recovery.

Since the characteristics of substance abuse are the same in the MRDD community, it is not surprising that they should also benefit from attendance at AA meetings. The literature seems to reflect assumptions, anecdotal evidence, concluding that AA meetings usually are not helpful for this population. While there is agreement that specialized treatment is needed with this population, it is possible that a stronger emphasis on the twelve-step programs might be beneficial. It is important to try to identify which aspects of the AA program are particularly helpful to MRDD individuals.

How the twelve steps enhance group work

Group work is defined by Kurland and Salmon (1992) as a way to work with people, that affirms their ability to contribute to others. By forming groups, we indicate that we believe that people do have strength and that they can help each other. While the process is guided by the worker in group work, the same elements are present in the twelve-step meeting, and work in the same way. The difference is that there is no leader to encourage the process. The premise of this paper is not to say that a twelve-step program is group work. It is only to say that the same principles of mutual aid guide both. Therefore, there is an opportunity to use the twelve-step programs a complement to treatment with the MRDD population, either by encouraging attendance at twelve step meetings, or using twelve step recovery principles and ideas within the group work context.

A key component both in group work and in the twelve-step programs is mutual aid. Mutual aid is defined as a force for development and change as the group practice builds on the interdependency of its members. (Northen & Kurland, 2001). Each participant gives and takes with the group, as they draw upon their own experience and desire to help fellow members. It builds self-esteem and increases a feeling of belonging to see that the sharing of your experience can be helpful to others. This is of crucial importance particularly in a population, which may have low self-esteem, and few avenues in which to build self-esteem.

Steinberg (2002) reinforces the idea of the group as a force for personal and political change. As she points out, when peers share ideas, feelings, attitudes, and personal stories to help each other get through situations, they provide space for new voices to speak and new possibilities to open up. That is what people do in twelve-step programs. They share their experience, strength, and hope, which opens up the space for others to engage in the same process. It may not work for everyone, but even the statistics show that very few addicts actually get clean and stay clean. The majority of those who achieve long term sobriety report long-term attendance in twelve-step programs. In terms of helping clients achieve and maintain sobriety, twelve-step programs are an important adjunct to therapy, if not the backbone of true recovery.

Mutual aid works both in twelve-step programs and other sobriety group work with this population: they complement each other. Self help, or mutual support, is the cornerstone of the anonymous programs, but is also operative in group work, and overlaps with the concept of mutual aid. In its simplest sense, it is the process of individuals in the group with a similar problem helping each other through the process of sharing information, thoughts, and feelings; and identifying with each other. Breton (1989) stressed that mutual aid is both healing and liberating, recognizing that the process through which members help each other is the power of the group. This leads to change, both for the individuals and for the group. The components of mutual aid demonstrated either in an AA meeting or group therapy at AHRC mirror those outlined by Shulman (1999): sharing data, the 'all in the same boat phenomena', developing a universal perspective, mutual support and demand, individual problem solving, rehearsal, and the strength in numbers phenomenon. While the process may be slower for the MRDD individual, it still unfolds in the same manner. It may follow a different cognitive route, but the basic process of change is the same. It only requires the ability to listen, hear, identify and learn. MRDD adults can also learn, it may be a slower or different process.

Another key concept is identification, defined by Northen and Kurland (2001) as a process where a person adopts an attitude, behavior, or value of another person, and integrates that new behavior or value into their own ego. As the group develops cohesiveness, positive identification takes place not only with other members but also with the group as an entity, and the values and norms of the group become incorporated into the members' personalities. In a simpler sense, someone in the group shares a story or experience, and the feelings that the experience produced. Other members identify with the feelings, if not the experience. This identification with both experience and feelings provides a basis for commonality, lessens isolation, and facilitates positive problem solving on a group basis, in this case, maintaining abstinence from substance abuse.

MRDD adults engage in the same process, they are not excluded because they cannot read or write, or may lack good memory skills. In both twelve-step programs and in group work at AHRC, the group coalesces, bonding takes place, members and the group move forward together. AA members have home groups, (a group that a member picks to attend regularly where they get to know other members and form relationships), sponsors (guides with long term sobriety), and both individual and group anniversaries. The group anniversaries reinforce continuity and growth even though they are completely voluntary and open-ended.

Power is another extremely important issue with this disempowered population. One of the benefits of AA is that there are no leaders, only 'trusted servants'. While members with long-term sobriety are respected, they do not govern or make decisions. Each group takes a 'group conscience' on various issues in a democratic process. All are welcome regardless of age, race, ethnicity, gender, sexual orientation, socioeconomic status, income, or level of education. The only requirement for membership is a desire to stop active substance abuse. The broad cross section of individuals who attend may make it more comfortable for the MRDD population as they see that people from all walks of life suffer from the disease of addiction, but also recover from it. Sometimes the lack of a leader who assumes authority for the direction of the group can be helpful – members are free to share whatever they need to share without judgment – there is no cross talk or feedback during meetings. This may be crucial for a feeling of safety and security in the group, especially for an MRDD adult, who may have been an object of ridicule for years.

Conclusion

Based on the experience at AHRC, this writer submits that like addiction, recovery from addiction is equal opportunity, and does not discriminate based on disability or the lack of disability. The process through which non-MRDD adults recover is just as available and accessible to MRDD adults, since essentially, it is a group mutual aid process, which happens through the collective experience of learning. Participants learn through the shared hope, strength, and experience of others recovering from addiction. It is through the telling of stories, identification, and reworking of one's own experience that the recovery takes place.

The twelve-step programs are free, and they are widely available and accessible. Realistically, MRDD adults require long term care on every level, including support for sobriety. Medicaid and other insurance companies will not pay for treatment indefinitely. Using the twelve-step concepts serves several purposes. Twelve-step recovery concepts are a natural fit with the mutual aid process, which is the backbone of our practice as group workers. The multiplicity of relationships involved in mutual aid – worker and group, worker and group members as individuals, and group members with each other – are reflected in the twelve-step concepts of sharing, identification, and growth, both for the group and each individual within the group. If the social work community recognizes and utilizes the benefit of twelve-step programs for the MRDD population, we will enrich our practices tremendously and strengthen the use of group work with this population.

References

American Psychiatric Association (1994). *Diagnostic and Statistical Manual of Mental Disorders (DSM-IV) (4ᵗʰ Ed.).* Washington, D.C.: American Psychiatric Association

Benshoff, J.J. (1990). Substance abuse: Challenges for rehabilitation. *Journal of Applied Rehabilitation Counseling,* 21(4), 9-12

Breton, M. (1989). Learning from social group work traditions. *Proceedings of the Eleventh Annual Symposium of Social Work with Groups.* Montreal, Canada

Burgard, J., Donohue, B., Azrin, N.H., and Teicher, G. (2000). Prevalence and treatment of substance abuse in the Mentally Retarded population: an empirical review. *Journal of Psychoactive Drugs,* 32(3), 293-298

Christian, L. and Poling, A. (1997). Drug abuse in persons with Mental Retardation: A review. *American Journal on Mental Retardation,* 102(2), 126-136

Connor, G.J., Tonigan, J.S., and Miller, W.R. (2001). A longitudinal model of intake symptomatology: AA participation and outcome: a retrospective study of the Project MATCH Outpatient and Aftercare Program. *Journal of Studies on Alcohol,* 62, 817-825

Davis, D.R. and Jansen, G.G. (1998). Making meaning of Alcoholics Anonymous for social workers: Myths, metaphors, and realities. *Social Work,* 43(2), 169-182

Delaney, D. and Poling, A. (1990). Drug abuse among mentally retarded people: An overlooked problem. *Journal of Alcohol and Drug Education,* 35, 48-54

Deloach, C.P. and Greer, B.G. (1981). *Adjustment to severe physical disability: A metamorphosis.* New York, NY: McGraw-Hill

Emrick, C.D. (1987). Alcoholics Anonymous: affiliation, process, and effectiveness as treatment. *Alcoholism: Clinical and Experimental Research,* 11, 416-423

Emrick, C.D., Tonigan, J.S., Montgomery, H.A., and Little, L. (1993). Alcoholics Anonymous: What is currently known? In B.S. McCrady and

W.R. Miuller (Eds.), *Research on Alcoholics Anonymous: Opportunities and alternatives. (*pp. 41-76). Piscataway, N.J.: Rutgers Center of Alcohol Studies

Frieden, A.L. (1990). Substance abuse and disability: the role of the independent living center. *Journal of Applied Rehabilitation Counseling,* 21(3), 33-36

Golden, H. (1992). *AHRC resource manual: Substance abuse and persons with mental retardation and developmental disabilities,* New York, NY: Sobriety Services Program, AHRC

Krischef, C.H. (1986). Do the mentally retarded drink? *Journal of Alcohol & Drug Education,* 31, 64-70

Krischef, C.H. and Dinitto, D.M. (1981). Alcohol abuse among mentally retarded individuals. *Mental Retardation,* 19, 151-155

Krischef, C.H. and Dinitto, D.M. (1984). Drinking patterns of mentally retarded people. *Alcohol Health & Research World,* 8(2), 40-42

Kurland, R. and Salmon, R. (1992). Group work vs. casework in a group: Principles and implication for teaching and practice. *Social Work With Groups,* 15(4), 3-14

Leech, T.B. (1992). A typology of the sponsor relationship in AA and other 12 step programs. *Rutgers, The State University of New Jersey PhD Thesis,* Source: DAI-A 54/03, p. 1094

Lottman, T.J. (1994). Access to generic substance abuse services for persons with Mental Retardation. *Journal of Alcohol & Drug Education,* 39(1), 41-55

McBride, J.L. (1991). Abstinence among members of Alcoholics Anonymous. *Alcoholism Treatment Quarterly,* 8, 113-121

Montgomery, H.A., Miller, W.R. and Tonigan, J.S.(1995). Does Alcoholics Anonymous involvement predict treatment outcome? *Journal of Substance Abuse Treatment,* 12, 241-246

Moore, D. and Polsgrove, L. (1991). Disabilities, developmental handicaps and substance misuse: A review, *International Journal of the Addictions,* 26, 65-90

Northen, H. and Kurland, R. (2001). *Social work with groups (3rd Ed.).* New York, NY: Columbia University Press

Paxon, J.E. (1995). Relapse prevention for individuals with developmental disabilities, borderline intellectual function, or illiteracy. *Journal of Psychoactive Drugs,* 27, 167-172

Peyrot, M. (1985) Narcotics Anonymous: Its history, structure, and approach. *The International Journal of the Addictions,* 20 (10), 1509-1522

Rappaport, J. (1993). Narrative studies, personal stories, and identity transformation in the mutual help context. *Journal of Applied Behavioral*

Science, 29, 239-256

Shipley, R.W., Taylor, S.T. and Falvo, D.R. (1990). Concurrent evaluation and rehabilitation of alcohol abuse and trauma. *Journal of Applied Rehabilitation Counseling,* 21(3), 37-39

Shulman, L. (1999). *The skills of helping individuals, families, groups, and communities (4ᵗʰ Ed.).* Itasca, Il.: F.E. Peacock

Small, J. (1980/81). Emotions Anonymous: counseling the mentally retarded substance abuser. *Alcohol Health Research World,* 5, 46

Smith, A. R. (1993). The social construction of group dependency in Alcoholics Anonymous. *Journal of Drug Issues,* 23, 689-704

Steinberg, D. M. (2002). The magic of mutual aid. *Social Work with Groups* ,25(1), 31-38

Thurstin, A.H., Alfano, A.M., and Sherer, M. (1986). Pretreatment MMPI profiles of AA members and non-members. *Journal of Studies on Alcohol,* 47(6), 468-471

Westermeyer, J., Kemp, K. and Nugent, S. (1996). Substance abuse among persons with mild mental retardation. *American Journal on Addictions,* 5: 23-31

Westermeyer, J. Phaobtong, C. and Neider, J. (1988). Substance use among mentally retarded persons: comparison of patients and a survey population. *Journal of Drug & Alcohol Abuse,* 14(1), 109-123

6
Group supervision:
Motivation for social action

Carol F. Kuechler and Jennifer Schwartz

Social work supervision has traditionally been a major form of training as well as a source of professional monitoring and development (Kadushin, 1992; Kaiser, 1997, Munson, 2002; Shulman, 1993). The primary focus of the supervisory relationship is the ethical and competent practice of social work with clients. While little is currently being written about the practice of *group supervision of professionals* in social work, particularly from the perspective of practitioners, group supervision as a modality is practiced in many social work settings (Holloway and Johnston, 1985; Prieto, 1996; Kuechler & Schwartz, 2002). A focus group study with practitioners was conducted to address this gap, emphasizing the group supervisor's experience with and perspectives on group supervision. Based on well-documented connections between group work and social action, supervisors were asked to identify any social action that had come from their supervision groups. This paper distinguishes unique aspects of group supervision, addresses the interconnectedness of social action, social group work, and supervision, and presents the social action activities reported by study participants in four focus groups conducted in the north and central mid-west and at the 24th Annual AASWG symposium held in Brooklyn, New York.

Group supervision

When the primary contract is supervision of practice, group supervision is distinguished from other models of group practice based primarily on contracts of consultation, coaching, or educating. This distinction is based on the definition of the supervisor-supervisee relationship as one of accountability (Barnard and Goodyear, 2000; Kadushin, 1977; 1992, Kaiser; 1997; Munson, 2002; Shulman, 1993; Weinbach, 2003). Kaiser (1997) notes that supervision by its nature heightens issues of power and authority, trust and vulnerability, in the context of fostering ethical practice and the ongoing development of professional skills. Supervisors, while not equal members in the realm of accountability, can moderate the impact of their positional and administrative power and authority by using group supervision (see, for example, Kadushin, 1992; Munson, 2002; Shulman, 1993; Weinbach, 2003). Functionally, group supervision has also been implemented as a way to address critiques that models of individual supervision foster dependency, to respond to efficiency and resource issues in agencies, and to provide cost-effective options for supervisees seeking licensure (e.g. Getzel and Salmon, 1977; Kadushin, 1992; Munson, 2002; Weinbach, 2003.)

Shulman (1993) and others note that the practice of supervision *in a group* poses unique challenges and issues for the supervisor and requires additional skills related to group leadership, balancing individual and group needs, and understanding group development and processes. In addition, the supervisees contribute to the supervisory process and ideally are 'actively involved in providing support and making demands' (Shulman, 1993, p. 225), thus reflecting the principles of the mutual aid process.

Challenges experienced in the practice of group supervision have been raised by practitioners (Kuechler & Schwartz, 2002) and scholars (see, for example, Munson, 2002) relative to the nature and limits of direct and vicarious liability. Other challenges related more specifically to the function of social action and the supervisory role, as well as the attainment of the knowledge and skills needed to support and implement social action, will be addressed later in the context of social action.

Despite these challenges, practitioners and supervisors, through the continued use of group supervision, model agreement with Getzel and Salmon (1985) who described group supervision as a 'positive approach in the [social workers'] professional organizational environment,' which, despite its challenges 'match[ed] the potential reward in humanizing and democratizing the workplace in these harsh and difficult times' (p.41). Their description of group supervision and its potential is congruent with group work, as the 'intentional work with a group of people, all of whom are equal members, where interaction occurs that not only influences individual members of the group to help themselves, but, in the process, to help each other in the group, the group as a whole and the larger society' (Andrews, 2003 p.1). In this context the potential for social action as an outcome of group work becomes the foundation for exploring social action and group supervision.

Social action and social group work

Throughout the history of the social work profession, social workers and their supervisors have been involved with issues of social justice (Munson, 2002; Brilliant, 1996; Haynes & Mickelson, 2000). Group work has historically been at the heart of social action work as exemplified by Jane Addams and the settlement house movement and Eduard Lindemann (Abramovitz, 1998). Haynes and Mickelson (2000) characterized three models of social action in use in the 1950s: 1) citizen social worker, 2) agent of social change, and 3) actionist. Two of these models, citizen social worker and actionist, relied heavily on group work to be effective. For example, the citizen social work model, 'calls for the profession of social work to use the information and knowledge gained through work with...groups to inform the larger society of the need for programs and policies' (Haynes and Mickelson, 2000, p. 10). Using the actionist model, social workers, with the client group, focused on bringing about desired change based on needs identified by the group members.

Regardless of the model of group work in use, it has often been demonstrated that it is unlikely for a group to develop without some form of injustice being identified, thus inviting the need for social action at some level. As noted by Getzel and Salmon (1985) and Cox (1991) social action is often not the primary focus of a group, but rather 'an integral and natural outcome of the mutual problem solving process in which [the group] engages' (Cox, p. 88). Breton (1995) likewise notes, 'any group has within itself the latent or unrealized capacity of moving its members to engage in social action and empowerment producing activities' (p. 5). The empowerment literature is likewise filled with examples of the social action activities accomplished by groups (for example, Bertcher, Kurtz, & Lamont, 1999; Lee, 1994) bringing to mind the oft used quote from Margaret Mead: *Never doubt that a small group of thoughtful citizens can change the world. Indeed, it is the only thing that ever has.*

Supervision and social action

Munson's (2002) view of supervision in the development of the profession provides the context for establishing a connection between supervision and social action. Starting with the premise that social reform, client advocacy, cost-effective interventions and an effective model of supervision are contributions made by social work to the helping professions; he characterized supervision as the 'glue that held together' the 'individual intervention, advocacy, and social reform that was the hallmark of the social work profession' (p. 87). He contextualizes this characterization by directing the reader to Mary Richmond's belief 'that reform, advocacy, and microintervention could be integrated by supervisors gathering data from supervisees and generating statistics that would be supplied to social reformers to influence philanthropists and legislators to meet social needs and promote prevention' (p. 87).

Gowdy and Freeman (1993) identify challenges faced by the supervisor in supporting social action within the agency context when the agency dynamics discourage 'sending up [complaints] through organizational channels' (p. 63). Wood and Middleman (1995) noted that social workers are at times limited in their social action engagement when *de facto* norms, i.e. operational procedures, discouraging social action are treated as *de jure* policies. When challenging these norms, social workers (and their supervisors) may be challenging societal norms as well as agency norms. Thus, when workers bring these issues to supervision, the importance of the supervisor's attitudes, skills and knowledge relative to change is heightened.

To the degree that social action involves change, the nature of change is understood and supported through the supervisory process. Shulman (1993) and Weinbach (2003) posit the expectation that social work supervisors and managers will encounter change at many levels in their work and that they need to be prepared to understand and deal with it. Understanding change is fundamental to their positions.

Change, regardless of the level of intervention, often raises the supervisory dilemma of balancing individual case needs with other demands. Gowdy and Freeman (1993) suggest that supervisors are unprepared to handle workers' feedback when its focus is other than case level issues. They point to gaps in supervisory methods, which blend program analysis and direct service. Breton (1995) cites the importance of knowing how to implement social action, suggesting that it is difficult for workers to adequately promote the ideas behind social action if they feel poorly educated or trained in the subject and that without the relevant skills and training 'any potential for social action will remain dormant' (p. 9). Brilliant (1986) suggested that supervisors, like many social workers are fundamentally not comfortable with the idea of social action and power. For the social worker, accessing supervisory support can be further challenged in situations where supervisors are not employed at the same organizations as their supervisees.

Examples of social action, which evolved from supervision groups, were reported by Gowdy and Freeman (1993). In their report on the effectiveness of program supervision, conducted in groups, they cited a number of social action-related outcomes. For example, they attributed the identification of hidden issues related to salary inequities and the emergence of program limitations to the group supervision process, which nurtured a secure and informal environment in contrast to the more formal individual supervision. The social actions noted were more likely to be based in the agency and its work, rather than in the broader sense of community-based change. In this context of the overlapping functions of: group supervision and social group work, social group work and social action, and supervision and social action, the potential for social action as an outcome of group supervision was explored in this study.

Method

A focus group design facilitated to address a specific research issue was selected as a model congruent with the research question with its emphasis on group process (Krueger, 1994). Participants (n=25) were recruited in Fall 2002 from current and past members of a continuing education program for community-based supervisors located in the Twin cities metropolitan area, from practitioners who belonged to or were recruited through an international group work organization in Kentucky and from participants at the organization's annual symposium in Brooklyn, New York. Focus groups lasted from one and a half to two and a half hours and were audio taped; longer sessions included a short break. Prior to the focus group process, participants completed a background information sheet (Berg, 2004), which included the main questions to be addressed such as inquiries about perceived benefits and challenges, frameworks of practice, social action activities emanating from supervision groups and recommendations for new practitioners.

Participants in four focus groups represented medical, school, social service, corrections, foster care, in-patient, and community counseling settings. Some were in private practice. Participants' experiences as group supervisors ranged from two weeks to thirty plus years. While all had practiced group supervision with practitioners, not all were currently practicing. One notable reason given for participating in the focus groups was the desire to find out what other people were doing as group supervisors.

Findings

When queried about social action activities and outcomes, some members readily described actions taken by their supervision groups. Others, who indicated that they had not identified any 'social action' on their background sheet, were prompted by the process to recall relevant examples. Not all examples of activities fit the notion of group action; some represented social actions taken by individual members of a particular supervision group. This paper focuses primarily on the group-based social action activities reported by the supervisors.

Group supervisors described a variety of social actions that emanated from the groups they supervised. Examples included actions within agencies that were client-related and those that were staff-related. The presentation of examples are organized on the basis of the content and focus of the social action described; the context of 'Agency-related' refers to the location of the action, not necessarily to the location of the supervision group. Client-related social action has been organized into three subcategories: advocacy, program development, and standardization (see Figure 1). Staff-related social action has four subcategories: empowerment, policy, staffing, and staff/professional development (see Figure 2).

Figure 1: Social Action Within Agencies: Client-Related

Advocacy
A change that occurred out of one of my groups was that materials were translated into Spanish...[the place the member worked] *was a drug and alcohol treatment center and the materials that they used were not in Spanish...and yet a lot of clients were Spanish speaking.*

In talking with staff and in supervision [there was discussion] *of the dual diagnosis issue...people were being treated for the primary issue of alcohol and drugs when we wanted to have a mental health contribution to the treatment process...that is changing now...*

...We are grant funded and every year the funding expired and Congress... didn't authorize the funding so we have been pretty good letter writers as a group [including getting other colleagues in the schools and community to write letters.] *We have done a pretty good job keeping track of legislation.*

Program Development
I supervised a group that were working in a level 5...EBD [Emotional Behavioral Disorders] *program for pretty behaviorally disturbed kids...*[members of the group discussed the challenges in the experience of these kids' transition to 7th grade]*...we were able to obtain funds from our special education department to actually take the kids on tours* [of their new school] *during the school year... there has also been talk in that group about writing a grant to promote some basketball activities* [for the kids].

People were sharing about several family situations and realized this group of families all lived in the same trailer park and all these little kids were being sexual with one another...[another member] *said she had done some community prevention work...and* [would] *present a proposal* [at the next meeting] *about what it would look like if we did some community thing* [in the trailer park] *So that came out of the sharing about what goes on in the supervisees' caseloads and that all the families happened to be in the same community*

Standardization

In the process of getting together and discussing common issues, [the group members] *realized that tardiness and absentee data was kept differently in every* [school]...*when we realized that this was a problem throughout the district we started talking about it with the principals. They were able to rewrite the rules about the truancy and tardiness and...I felt very, very good about the process. It definitely came out of the group getting together and realizing that there was a problem and then deciding to do something about it.*

The workers that I am supervising at the behavioral health setting have... instituted some policies about...treatment planning for group members...and really trying to get a screening tool...for who might be good for working within groups. They have kind of done that on their own as an outgrowth [of the group].

Figure 2: Social Action Within Agencies: Staff-Related

Empowerment

...*my team has challenged policies at my agency...they feel like they can have* [the]...*voice to disagree with me and challenge the...larger agency.*

I found [what] *the group has been able to do, in a really powerful way, is to assist* [the supervisees] *to go back to the agency* [to challenge an abusive situation] *and not put their job at risk.*

Policy

...*one of the supervisees brought a policy change when* [the directors of a new program were] *making management statements around sexual orientation and prohibition in...allowing homosexuals intake* [into the agency]. *I saw...the agency as* [a] *client as well...We practiced in the group...how he would approach the board...he used us as a sounding board...he did challenge the board and created all kinds of media coverage.*

[Supervisees identified] *that one of the greatest sources of frustrations for them was staff turnover...we looked...hard at those issues and then put forward recommendations for improvements in their working conditions and increases in the pay for the frontline people...*[also the group] *created equity in the salary structure and the assignment of titles based on responsibilities in the organization.*

Staffing

One of the [supervision] *groups I was in demoted their supervisor...they said that 'we are not accepting you as a supervisor anymore'...he was also their administrative supervisor...I think it is really important to have everybody working on it together...*

In the agency I worked for, one of the staff was fired because of her sexual orientation...it was a big group process...she [the person who was fired] *had been part of my supervision group...they asked me to fire her and I wouldn't do it...in the group process of talking with the* [other] *people I supervise... their first reaction was 'what are you going to do about this?'* [As a result of the circumstances the supervisor speaking here resigned rather than fire the supervisee.]

Staff/Professional Development

...as a result of some of our group supervision [the supervisees] *got more training on topic areas that they need training around.*

...[Respondent's supervisees] *went out on their own and* [got] *more training because they knew they were lacking in certain areas that they wanted to be skilled...*[they] *brought people into the agency to provide training.*

Sometimes the need for additional training [for agency-related work] *has come from the group.*

Discussion

These examples, which represent contributions from over half of the study participants, exemplify the power of groups to effect change in the context of group supervision conducted in a variety of agency and practice settings. Although the context for social action and change in most of the examples was the agency or organization itself, many of the client-related activities (Figure 1) had a broader impact in the community. For example, materials translated into Spanish were made available for future clients and could facilitate access to services; education offered in the community was available to non-clients as well as those on the caseloads of the social workers; and standardized policies about tardiness and absentee data facilitated communication between schools. Getzel and Salmon (1985) noted, 'although the primary purpose of group supervision is not the explicit alteration of organizational activities, it may be a latent function' (p.41). The examples provided by the diverse array of 'group supervisors' who participated in this study demonstrate the reality of this statement. While the focus of their supervisory groups was not to 'create change', their stories exemplify the power and energy of practitioners working together in a safe and supportive environment.

These findings exemplify how the premise presented that social action may be inherent in any type of group (Getzel and Salmon, 1985; Cox, 1991; Breton, 1995) can be true for supervision groups as well. For over half of our respondents an opportunity for social action developed from their supervision group. In these examples, the supervisors functioned in their group leadership role to guide and support the social actions and in their 'third force' (Shulman, 1993) role as effective mediators between the workers and the agency administration. Using their examples and guidance from the literature, we present some strategies for supervisors who wish to open their supervisory guidance to the realm of social action.

The strategies are divided into three categories: 1) supervisor-focused, 2) group-focused, and 3) worker-focused, though all are presented for action by the supervisor. Documentation for these strategies is grounded in the literature and is congruent with input from the study participants as reported in segments of the transcripts not reported in this paper.

Strategies for supervisors to support social action

Supervisor-focused

- View the task environment as a resource (Weinbach, 2003)
- Become a resource person (Cox, 1991, Toseland, 1995)
- Address the power differentials in supervisor-supervisee relationship through participative management (Cox, 1991; Toseland, 1995; Weinbach, 2003)
- Model openness to sharing power, authority and knowledge (Shulman, 1993; Weinbach, 2003)
- Engage in self-examination relative to social action (Colwell, 2001)
- Model involvement in collective or social action (Porter, 1994)

Group-focused

- Facilitate the mutual aid process in the group (Shulman, 1993)
- Facilitate linkages and communication between the group and change agents in the community (Cox, 1991; Toseland, 1995)
- Share power and allow leadership to come from within the group (Cox, 1991; Toseland, 1995)
- Create an organizational climate for teamwork, risk-taking, and openness to change (Porter, 1994)

Worker-focused

- Understand and support the process of change (Lewin, 1951 as cited in Shulman, 1993; Weinbach, 2003)
- Facilitate the development of worker skills in communication, mediation and advocacy (Cox, 1991; Toseland, 1995)
- Hold and share a vision for hope with enthusiasm (Gitterman and Shulman, 1986; Breton, 1995)
- Be proactive in supporting supervisee involvement in the process of change at all levels of practice

Conclusion

The findings of this study demonstrate a strong connection between group supervision and social action. This connection is grounded in the interrelated historical roots of social group work and social work supervision. None of the agencies represented by the group supervisors in this study have social action as a primary service mission, yet over half of the respondents were parties to a variety of social action situations in their supervision groups. The reality of this experience suggests that supervisors need to be prepared in attitude, knowledge and skill to guide supervisees in the natural social action outcomes of the group supervision process.

References

Abramovitz, M. (1998) Social work and social reform: An arena of struggle. *Social Work, 43*(6), 512-526

Andrews, J. (September 2003). The historical connection between social group work and social justice. Presented at The Annual Meeting and Membership Event of the Association for the Advancement of Social Work with Groups - Minnesota Chapter: *Social justice and the power of group work*. Jewish Community Center, St. Paul, MN.

Berg, B.L. (2004). *Qualitative research methods for the social sciences*, 5th Ed.. Boston: Allyn Bacon.

Bernard, J.M. and Goodyear, R.K.. (1998). *Fundamentals of clinical supervision, 2nd ed.* Boston: Allyn & Bacon.

Bertcher, H., Kurtz, L. F, and Lamont, A. (Eds). (1999) *Rebuilding communities: Challenges for group work*. New York: Haworth Press.

Breton, M. (1995). The potential for social action in groups. *Social Work with Groups, 18* (2/3), 5-13.

Brilliant, E. (1986). Social work leadership: A missing ingredient? *Social Work*, September/October, 325-330.

Colwell, J. (2001). Beyond brainstorming: How managers can cultivate creativity and creative-problem solving skills in employees. *Supervision*, 62 (8), 6-9.

Cox, E.O. (1991). Critical role of social action in empowerment oriented groups. *Social Work with Groups 14* (3/4) 77-90.

Getzel, G.S., Goldberg, J.R., and Salmon, R. (March 1971). Supervising in groups as a model for today. *Social Casework*, 154-163.

Getzel, G.S. and Salmon, R. (1985). Group supervision: An organizational approach. *The Clinical Supervisor, 3*(1), 27-43.

Gitterman, A. and Shulman, L. (1986). *Mutual aid groups and the life cycle*. Itasca, NY: F.E. Peacock.

Gowdy, E. and Freeman, E. (1993). Program supervision: Facilitating staff participation in program analysis, planning, and change. *Administration in Social Work, 17*(3), 59-79.

Haynes, K.S. and Mickelson, J.S. (2000). *Affecting change: Social workers in the political arena (4th ed.)*. Needham Heights, MA: Allyn & Bacon.

Holloway, E.L. and Johnston, R. (1985). Group supervision: Widely practices but poorly understood. *Counselor Education and Supervision, 24*, 332-340.

Kadushin, A. (1977). *Consultation in social work*. New York: Columbia University Press.

Kadushin, A. (1992). *Supervision in social work 3rd ed*. New York: Columbia University Press.

Krueger, R.A. (1994). *Focus groups: A practical guide for applied research*, 2nd Ed. Thousand Oaks, CA: SAGE Publications.

Kuechler, C. F., and Schwartz, J. (October 2002). *Group supervision or supervision in a group? A focus group study*. Presented at the Twenty-Fourth International Symposium of the Association for the Advancement Of Social Work with Groups. *Think Group: Strength and Diversity in Group Work*. New York City, NY.

Lee, J.A. (1994). *The empowerment approach to social work practice*. New York: Columbia University Press.

Lowry, L. (1992). Social group work with elders: Linkages and intergenerational relationships. *Social Work with Groups, 15*(2/3), 109-127.

Munson, C.E. (2002). *Handbook of clinical social work supervision*, 3rd Ed. Binghampton, NY: The Haworth Social Work Practice Press.

Porter, N. (1994). Empowering supervisee to empower others: A culturally responsive supervision model. *Hispanic Journal of Behavioral Sciences, 16*(1), 43-56.

Prieto, L. R. (1996). Group supervision: Still widely practiced but poorly understood. *Counselor Education and Supervision, 35*(4), 295-307.

Shulman, L. (1993). *Interactional supervision*. Washington, D.C.: NASW Press.

Toseland, R. W. (1995). *Group work with the elderly*. New York: Springer Publishing Company.

Weinbach, R.W. (2003). *The social worker as manager: A practical guide to success, 4th ed*. Boston: Allyn & Bacon.

Wood, G.G. and Middleman, R.R. (1991). Advocacy and social action: Key elements in the structural approach to direct practice in social work. *Social Work with Groups. 14*(2/3), 53-63

7

'As if by magic':
Women with breast cancer, dragon boats and healing in a group

Paule McNicoll

Many women with breast cancer continue to experience psychological difficulties after they have been cleared of cancer through treatment, usually a mix of surgery, chemotherapy and radiation. (Andersen, Anderson and deProsse, 1989; Andersen, Kiecolt-Glaser and Glaser, 1994). They have lived multiple traumatic experiences including the diagnosis of cancer, major life disruptions, nausea and fatigue inducing treatments and uncertainty. The psychological consequences of cancer include: depression, anxiety disorders, post-traumatic stress symptoms (Cordova, Andrykowski, Kenady, McGrath, Sloan and Redd, 1995), appetite disturbances (Wellisch, Wolcott, Pasnau, Fawzy and Lansverk, 1989), and chronic sleep disorders (Cella and Tross, 1986). Contact with health care professionals, which at times had surpassed contact with family and friends, tend to end abruptly once the cancer is gone. The message is: 'Now, you are better. Take this pill regularly. Go home'. The ex-patient feels abandoned with her incredulity, continuing fears, anxiety, and grief over the losses of the last year or so. Her cancer journey is not over, yet it is perceived to be so. Acquaintances, friends and family expect her to be ecstatic, and therefore her pain is not seen as legitimate. Deep loneliness, depression and immobilization can be consequences of this state of affairs.

When lucky and/or wise, a woman will join a group of others who have lived through the same experience as herself. Support groups

This paper was written in close collaboration with Kate Doyle and the original crew of Abreast in a Boat. Paule McNicoll was the sole presenter at the Boston Symposium, but she considers her partners as full co-authors of this chapter.

(Gore-Felton and Spiegel, 1999), group psychotherapy (Spiegel, Bloom and Yalom, 1981; Spira and Reed, 2003) and group psychoeducation (Devine and Westlake, 1995) have been the first interventions recognized as helpful for women facing cancer. In the last few years, these groups have been supplemented by stress management (Stanton and Reed, 2002), meditation (Angen, MacRae, Simpson and Hundleby, 2002; Massion, Teas, Hebert, Wertheimer and Kabat-Zinn, 1995), art and creative therapies (Hundleby, Robson, Cumming, Kieren and Handman, 1998), dream work (Goelitz, 2001), and exercise (Andersen et al., 1994; Segar, Katch, Roth, Weinstein Garcia, Portner, Glickman, Haslanger and Wilkins, 1998).

This chapter presents the findings of a qualitative study with a group of women who have had cancer. When they came together, these women only expected to participate in a medical experiment and disband thereafter. On their way, however, they were surprised to find friendship, fun, support, joy, pleasure, power and healing. Recognizing their experience as too precious to be kept for themselves, these women invited the first author to collaborate with them to identify the 'magic' that had transformed their lives.

It all started when this group of women volunteered to participate in a study about exercise and the risk of lymphedema in women with a history of breast cancer. The conservative medical position at the time was to instruct post-surgery patients to avoid strenuous activity to prevent lymphedema, a nasty side effect of cancer treatment. (McKenzie, 1998). The study volunteers were required to exercise regularly as members of a dragon boat[1] team and the effect of exercise was monitored weekly by medical practitioners. (A dragon boat is a long and narrow boat with a prow in the form of a dragon. It is propelled by 22 paddlers who are following the rhythm of one drummer and are steered by one navigator).

Fortunately, no one developed lymphedema, and all had the satisfaction of having contributed to debunking the myth that women had to avoid upper-body exercise after surgery. Moreover, the group participated in a Dragon Boat race. While mere participation was seen as a victory, they were elated when they discovered that they were not finishing last, as expected. The group, named *Abreast in a Boat,* also attracted much media attention, something they eventually found to their liking.

When they were expected to disband as a group after the completion of the study, the women refused. They argued that they had experienced an 'incredible uplifting of [their] mood', 'wonderful feelings of friendship and warmth', and a myriad of potent physical, social and emotional benefits. Within a few months of their paddling, some women who had needed antidepressants had stopped taking them; others who had prior group experience mentioned that their participation in the exercise study brought greater support and more positive factors in their lives than the standard support groups for survivors of cancer to which they still belonged. These arguments won over their coaches who agreed to continue working with them, and to even expand the Dragon Boat fleet to other teams of women with breast cancer. It's at this point that we decided to join forces to try understanding the 'magic' that had happened to them and to 'bottle it' for others, if possible.

To explore the social processes that contributed to this enhanced well-being, we held five group meetings over three years. The study was not funded and it often took long periods of time before volunteer participants could transcribe the data and the feedback from the meetings. The meetings were held in some of the women's homes and were occasions for potluck dinners. Most of the data were gathered during the two first meetings, while the three last meetings focused on data analysis. During the data-gathering period, members responded to the questions prepared by the first two authors. They also answered a short questionnaire about their experience with the team. Because we are a big group, we tried to divide the first meetings into two sittings, but all members showed up on the first occasion, and we abandoned the practice.

The three meetings that focused on analysis consisted in presentations of initial findings, in a general discussion of these findings as to whether they were representing fairly the experience shared by members, and in responses to detailed questions prepared by the two first authors, who also had worked on the preliminary findings. All meetings were audiotaped. The transcribed content of these groups and the responses to the short anonymous written questionnaire were analyzed using the constant comparison approach (Strauss and Corbin, 1998). We identified and categorized themes based on their breadth (all women talked independently about all themes) and depth (themes were ordered based on recurrence and emphasis).

Findings

First Analysis: Nine themes

A first series of findings led to the uncovering of nine themes, presented here by order of importance. Each theme was supported by a series of very moving quotes from the participants. For space's sake, we provide only one quote under each theme. However, all nine themes were endorsed by all members as representative of their experience.

1. **Connection, cohesion**
   The unison, and the effect, and the common success, it is almost that there was some communication that was more than verbal.

2. **Receiving and providing support**
   It's been neat having all the family support ... all the husbands, kids, friends.

   There's a part of me that wants to ally the fears of my friends and family...for me it was a way of saying: 'you see, I'm okay'.

3. **Cancer experience**
   What the team did for me was let me accept that I had cancer.

4. **Public experience, media attention**
   ... and doing this for fun and for breast cancer people and for ourselves and everything, but the success of [the public relations], I think, astounded us.

5. **Exercise, exertion, challenge**
   It is also very important, and unusual, to have a comfortable and safe place to push myself physically.

6. **Fun, excitement, enthusiasm, positive attitude**
   Paddling with Abreast in a Boat allows me to keep a promise I made to myself when I found I had breast cancer. To have fun; to be with people who understand the importance of fun; to spend as little time as possible with people who do not understand the above.

7. Competitiveness

... and we beat the lawyers ... and before we beat them, they were saying: 'Good for you, ladies!' ... People were very sort of patronizing ... it was just great for us to be out there ... a lot of 'ladies'...and no one expected us to actually beat anyone else. Well, we didn't. We didn't either expect to. We were just excited to just finish the race ... it was the wind...we became much more competitive after, when we saw ... it became much more of a possibility that we actually could beat other people ... then we REALLY wanted to beat other people.

8. Positive spin, turning negative into positive

It has been great. It has helped me turn a terrible situation - the diagnosis of cancer - into a positive experience. It has enriched my life - a new sport, new friends, travel, confidence once again in my body and a healing process for my mind.

9. Mystical, transcendental experience, water

The physical setting was unbelievable. No matter what else in your life was going on, if you're busy working or feeling great or not feeling great or frightened or positive, you would get down there on a Wednesday evening in the spring in Vancouver and suddenly it was like crossing a bridge and you see these people that were going to do the same thing, kind of a ritual almost, get your paddle, life jacket and get into position, and then there would be wild talking for a while and then you'd get the boat on the water...honestly, False Creek in the middle of the summer, what more would you want, the days were getting nicer and we'd fool around for a few minutes and then bang, we would be in unison paddling down that beautiful stretch...it's pretty special. It's kind of a spiritual thing.

These findings were discussed by the members of the dragon boat team. The women expressed satisfaction with the results, making minor corrections speaking even more eloquently about their experience. Although proud of our work, we were still not satisfied that we had really captured the 'magic' the women had experienced. We decided to have a longitudinal look at the data and came up with the following results.

Second analysis: A trajectory

- **Preliminary doubts**
  general: shyness
  specific: - *'I'm not a jock'*
              - some will have recurrence

- **Motivating factors and expected rewards**
  Connection with other women
  Fun (including temporary liberation from daily tasks)
  Exercise
  Healing from trauma
  Knowledge on health and strength post-surgery
  Speaking for other women with breast cancer

- **Unexpected experiences**
  Rewards: Reassurance of friends and family
                New state of wellness
                Public attention
                Safety net in case of recurrence
                Positive research outcome
                Pride (athletic achievement)
                Finding of true friends
                Coming to terms with existential reality

- **Group process difficulties**
  Conflict over competition. Some women wanted to emphasize cohesion and support among members of the crew while others wanted the team to become a serious contender for winning Dragon Boat races. While these goals are not completely at odds with each other, the difference of focus meant that there were tense discussions about many day-to-day decisions.

- **Conclusion:**
  Lack of team sports opportunities for adult women

Once again, these findings were discussed at a meeting of all 'Abreast in a Boat' members who recognized them to correspond to their experience. The only objections had to do with the expression that 'cancer softens personality', something written to convey the idea that cancer helped members to clarify their life priorities and make it less likely that they would engage in petty disputes. The expression was subsumed under 'a new state of wellness' to convey women's sense that they had gained focus and flexibility as well as strength and balance.

While interesting, these findings are descriptive and do not help, in themselves, to determine whether we are in presence of a lucky accident or something that can be reproduced. These findings also do not permit us to identify the 'magic' element(s) that contributed to the women's transformation. At this point, we became curious about the idea of looking at metaphors within the transcripts of our meetings. In particular, we noticed participants' vivid presentation of their experience. They talked about their fear of '*sinking* in sadness' and subsequently of belonging to a '*floating* support group' (our italics). We presented our idea for a new analysis of the data focusing on metaphors to a few members of the group; they accepted enthusiastically. This technique of working with data is similar to schema analysis, as presented by Ryan and Bernard (2000). In a first step, a constant comparison approach was used to identify all recurrent metaphors. Axial and selective coding of these metaphors then led to the uncovering of a network of psychosocial tasks whose successful completion was facilitated by the Dragon Boat experience.

Third analysis: Metaphors of psychosocial tasks

Thus, the third analysis of the data unfurled at three levels: 1. Psychosocial tasks women felt they needed to address, 2. Dragon Boat experiences corresponding to each task, and 3. Outcome. There are three levels of tasks: personal, familial and social.

Most of the tasks were situated at the personal level. There were two major personal tasks: one, to come to terms with the experience of cancer and to move on with life, and the other, to re-experience one's body as a place of strength and pleasure.

Personal Level

First task: To come to terms with the experience of cancer and to move on with life.

This involved five sub-tasks.

1. First, one had to fight the popular overdramatic and tragic connotations of cancer. The experience of participating in the Dragon Boat race established a linkage of cancer with a positive connotation.

    Well, it's great because you say breast cancer and then you say Dragon Boat or trekking in Nepal or whatever.

    The outcome was an integration of cancer in daily life.

    And it's the scary part, and then there's life.

2. The second sub-task was to overcome loneliness.

    Going through the breast cancer experience is lonely. You may have your best friends on either side of you, but still you're in there by yourself, with that machine, or chemo, or whatever it is, by yourself, and it's very lonely.

    The experience required paddling in unison

    We really worked together to have the timing, to stay together...so that was the important thing...working together.

    The outcome was strong group cohesion

    When one of our members had a recurrence, the whole group came together to see what we could do for her and I thought: 'Wow! If something happened to me, I sure would like to think that there is a group out there for me that would at least phone or at least know what I might be going through.' It really meant...it has made this group way more important than just a Dragon Boat team.

3. A third sub-task was to deal with the fear of *'sinking down in sadness'*.

    The essence of the paddling experience is staying afloat, moving *on* water. The outcome for the women was the creation of a *'floating support group'*.

4. A fourth sub-task was to face the possibility of recurrence.
    Statistically with a group that size, there will be someone who will
    have recurrences and how, from a self-centered point of view, how
    will that affect me?

    The experience placed cancer squarely in their consciousness.

    Breast cancer is the admission fee to the Club.

    The outcome was that they could be upfront together and together
    face uncertainty.

    It's a great analogy for life, too, pulling together and being in the same
    boat, being upfront.

5. The fifth sub-task was to face the facts fully and in depth.
    I've had breast cancer for 18 years and I had a new tumor 3 years ago,
    so I've sort of had the treatment recently and treatment a long time
    ago and when I was diagnosed, I didn't want to have anything to do
    with breast cancer and I didn't want to talk about it.

    The experience provided by the Dragon Boat team was the
    opportunity to share with other women who had breast cancer in
    a context where breast cancer is not the central experience. The
    metaphor is important: *'All in the same boat'*

    I didn't go there to make friends, it wasn't my goal. I wanted to get
    physically fit with more of a personal challenge and to actually learn
    some skills, and have some fun.

    ... because you're in the boat and your practice was in the boat and
    obviously when you're paddling you can't really be talking to each other,
    although we developed that skill (laughter).

    ... it started happening maybe at the mandatory practices when we
    had to hang around.

    ... there were little meetings after the paddling practices... where we
    would sit around on the grass and chat. I mean, it wasn't talking about
    the kids, it was talking and it was social contact, and it got longer and
    longer.

    ... even though initially nobody really talked about their experiences
    with breast cancer, it was almost like we were soul mates because we
    all had gone through this together. We all knew.

    The outcome was an integration of positive and negative aspects
    of cancer.

For me the experience [of cancer] has been a difficult one but it hasn't been a sad one...once you get over the tears, which still come...it's been a really valuable experience and I wanted to share that and I've never really had anybody that I could share it with. (Participant who had cancer recently)

A participant who had cancer twice stated:

However I had dealt with it [the first time around], it wasn't over, that's for sure. I needed another dimension to it to accept it. What the team did for me was let me accept that I had cancer ... because up until that time, I felt really angry and quite frightened and I didn't know a lot of women with it.

Second task at the personal level: to re-experience one's body as a site of strength and pleasure.

For this, women needed to conquer the fear of using their bodies.

I was shocked there was a whole list of things I was never ever supposed to do again. I kept hearing all the warnings about using the arm so I was scared to use my arm but I had to use my arm if I was to continue doing my kind of work so it was a struggle to work all that out... I was really conscious of it. Anytime I would lift groceries, I would use the other arm... It was always in the back of my mind.

Participants on the Dragon Boat team experienced exercising in safety.

It was so reassuring to see everyone else with their arms measured that I would think: 'Oh, I can do it next week'.

The outcome was power and pleasure.

There is that moment when you're gliding and you think: 'OOOH'. It's a great feeling. It really gave me an increased sense of confidence because I was relatively close to my surgery...so I was very vulnerable...I felt the Dragon Boat team, there were times when I felt quite powerful and I think that quite independent of breast cancer, there are lots of times women feel not very powerful and we were all paddling together and the boat was really moving and we passed the other boat, I had a sense of POWER.

Familial Level

This task involved healing with family and friends.

> *...you don't get the support you should really get sometimes unless someone has really gone through it.*

The Dragon Boat experience provided a clear and easy supportive role to family members and friends.

> *It's been an easy way for them to talk about breast cancer. 'My wife is on this Dragon Boat team and all those women have breast cancer.' 'Breast cancer? They look like they're having fun, they look okay...' It's a reassurance for them. It made it a possible topic. Before it was too sad... they'd probably been able to give support, but not known how.*

The outcome was that women felt supported and family and friends felt they could play an effective supportive role.

> *What Tom said was, and he sees himself as a groupie, he follows us around ...*
> *Albert is sort of like a border collie. He would like to run around the edges, making sure that everyone is okay.*

Social Level

At the social level, women intended to break the silence around breast cancer

> *It's always been sort of hidden...you never talked about it. A generation ago, women died but you weren't sure how.*

The experience of wearing a hot-fuchsia t-shirt with 'Abreast in a Boat' written across it made their position very visible. The outcome was local, national and international publicity and the starting of more than 90 teams.

> *The cameras were there time after time after time ...*
> *That was the icing on the cake and it was a wonderful acknowledgment*

and recognition that we were really doing something, something important.

These are a few of the metaphors that emerged through the analysis. We keep discovering new ones, such as when one of us attended a conference on qualitative research and noticed a drawing made by a Chinese-Canadian woman who had survived breast cancer: she had drawn herself riding on a dragon! (Hundleby, Robson, Cumming, Kieren and Handman, 1998). The participants endorsed these last findings as the ones that most represented their experience. To add a theoretical explanation of 'the magic' to the descriptive images the data procured, we borrowed from adventure therapy (e.g., Outward Bounds) theory. One of the tenets of that theory is that people can learn in three ways: *specific transfer,* which indicates the direct learning of a skill such as paddling; *non-specific transfer,* which relates to the acquisition of indirect principles associated with the specific learning, for instance, cooperation; and the third one of interest in this paper, *metaphoric transfer,* which happens when a direct learning experience parallels, in form and outcome, another aspect of the learner's life (Gass, 1991). There seems to have been metaphorical linkages between emotional tasks to heal from cancer and components of the Dragon Boat experience that have similar structures and present opportunities to complete the emotional tasks at a deeper level. Figure 1 illustrates how metaphoric transfer may happen from the addition of a positive experience (Dragon boat team) to a negative one (cancer) and a difficult task, the strong binding of the person to the positive experience, and the progressive distance established with the negative one.

When working through metaphors, one bypasses people's conscious defense mechanisms (Erickson, 1980; Haley, 1973). It is quick and thoroughly effective, in group work as well as in work with individuals (Sunderland, 1997-98; Duffy, 2001). Metaphors may be an ideal medium for working with groups of people with cancer who tend to avoid addressing issues of death and dying directly (Gore-Felton and Spiegel, 1999). Other indirect ways of addressing life-and-death issues, such as dream work, also tend to be more acceptable and beneficial to people (Goelitz, 2001).

With hindsight, all three analyses proved useful, each pointing to different dimensions of the experience. While three analyses emphasized the importance of cohesion, it is the first one that establishes its preponderance in relation to other factors. During the constant comparison analysis, we found two and a half times as many

Figure 1
Dragon boat team therapeutic process through metaphoric transfer

| Dragon boat team experience | Post cancer life tasks | Sequelae of cancer experience |

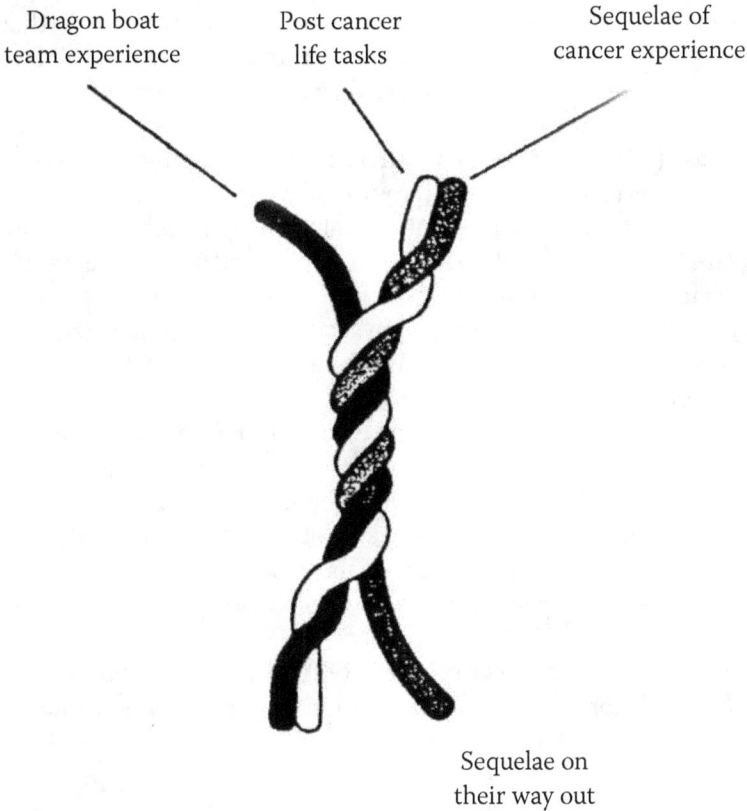

Sequelae on
their way out

Adapted from Gass, 1991, p. 7. Published with permission of the *Journal of Experiential Education*

data related to cohesion in the transcripts as for the second most important theme: receiving and providing support. Cohesion is the soul of social group work. These results support that what was really at play in the 'magic' was a central component of social work with groups. Moreover, if it weren't for the thematic analysis, we would have missed the 'awe' factor, the connection between the beauty and 'strangeness' of the setting and the deep reflection on existence, meaning and spirituality.

This last factor relates to an important aspect of adventure therapy: the requirement of an unfamiliar setting (Powch, 1994). There is a spiritual dimension to being in wilderness, in close contact with nature (Powch, 1994). Kiewa (1994), noting that not all wilderness adventures are positive, presents eight (8) characteristics that are present in the positive experiences. The first four are essential factors for a positive experience: an experiential approach, a simple and meaningful reality, need for cooperation, and intensity of feelings. The last four factors are facultative, but highly facilitative: processing of the experience (provided in our case by the study), success, choice of participation, and a humane climate. All eight factors were present in the experience of Abreast in a Boat. In setting up their scientific experiment, Dr. McKenzie may have inadvertently constructed an experience that paralleled the physical, emotional and spiritual tasks that these survivors of breast cancer needed to complete their journey through illness.

The second analysis ends on an exhortation for the creation of more team sport opportunities for women. 'Team' refers to the potential for group cohesion. 'Sport' refers to exercise. Exercise is a proven remedy for depression and anxiety. However, it is clear in the three analyses that, while a potent component of the 'magic' experienced by women in the group, it played a secondary role in respect to cohesion and metaphorical learning.

These results support Breton's (1990) call for a return to social work group traditions, especially in relation to the recreation movement. They challenge us to explore new and dynamic approaches to group work. They particularly challenge the usual style of group presentation, where members are invited as victims and survivors instead of pioneers and innovators. A different twist on presentation may help solve the most basic group problem: attracting members. In particular, such an approach may attract groups of people who do not find verbal exchanges alone to be particularly pleasant or useful.

Conclusion

The women of the Dragon Boat team faced an existential crisis and metaphorical learning facilitated not only a resolution to that crisis but the creation of a strong web of support, a community. There were recurrences, even deaths. But, to this day, the bonds remain intact and include not only members, but their close families as well. Here are a few quotes recorded at our last meeting, three years after the beginning of our collective search for 'magic'.

I don't know how I would have got through this year without you...It is such a comfort to me to know that if something happens, my family has all of you. (Participant who had a recurrence)

My daughter lost the sight in her eye last year, which was awful...the reason she could deal with it as well was because of my team...She had to have some terrible surgery and we were in the darkened hotel room after when some flowers were delivered. She looked over and she said: 'I bet they are from my paddling aunties'.

Life situations can be so sad and painful that a direct stare into them can be overwhelming, precluding understanding and action. Metaphors offer an alternative pathway, permitting a tangential approach, the introduction of healthy and positive elements in the picture, the alleviation of raw pain and the possibility of a gentler, easier resolution.

Group workers always keep an eye on individual group members, the group as a whole and the environment. At the environmental level, there are obstacles to the creation of groups that work mainly through metaphorical transfer. We live in a modern culture that increasingly enforce notions of directness, cognition, expert knowledge, focus on problems, standardization and accountability. Since, more and more, corporate entities, the holders of this culture, are paying the bill, these various notions come to spell CONTROL. We will need to be creative, subversive and/or persuasive to establish groups that 'access other intelligences' (Lang, 2003) as efficient and legitimate.

References

Andersen, B. L., B. Anderson, and C. deProsse (1989). Controlled prospective longitudinal study of women with cancer: II. Psychological outcomes. *Journal of Consulting and Clinical Psychology,* 57: 692-697.

Andersen, B. L., J. K. Kiecolt-Glaser, and R. Glaser (1994). A behavioral model of cancer stress and disease course. *American Psychologist,* 49: 389-404.

Angen, M. J., J. H. MacRae, J. S. Simpson, and M. Hundleby (2002). Tapestry: A retreat program of support for persons living with cancer. *Cancer Practice, 10* (6): 297-304.

Breton, M. (1990). Learning from social work group traditions. *Social Work with Groups, 13* (3), 21-34.

Cella, D. F. and S. Tross (1986). Psychological adjustment to surival from Hodgkin's disease. *Journal of Consulting and Clinical Psychology, 54:* 616-622.

Cordova, M. J., M. A. Andrykowski, D. E. Kenady, P. C. McGrath, D. A. Sloan, and W. H. Redd (1995). Frequency and correlates of posttraumatic-stress-disorder-like symptoms after treatment for breast cancer. *Journal of Consulting and Clinical Psychology, 63:* 981-986.

Devine, E. C. and S. K. Westlake (1995). The effects of psychoeducational care provided to adults with cancer: Meta-analysis of 116 studies. *Oncology Nursing Forum, 22:* 1369-1381.

Duffy, T. K. (2001). White gloves and cracked vases: How metaphors help group workers construct new perspectives and responses. *Social Work with Groups, 24,* 3/4: 89-99.

Gass, M. (1993). *Adventure therapy: Therapeutic applications of adventure programming.* Dubuque, Iowa: Kendall/Hunt Publishing Company. [Book]

Gass, M. (1991). Enhancing metaphor development in adventure therapy programs. *The Journal of Experimental Education, 14,* 2: 6-13.

Goelitz, A. (2001). Dreaming their ways into life: A group experience with oncology patients. *Social Work with Groups, 24,* 1: 53-67.

Gore-Felton, C. and D. Speigel (1999). Enhancing women's lives: The role of support groups among breast cancer patients. *Journal for Specialists in Group Work, 24,* 3: 274-287.

Hundleby, M., M. Robson, C. Cumming, D. Kieren, and M. Handman (1998). The challenge of breast cancer: The inside story from supportive-expressive therapy groups. Paper presented at the 4rth International Multidisciplinary Qualitative Health Research Conference. Vancouver, British Columbia, February 19-21.

Erickson, M. H. (1980). *The collected papers of Milton H. Erickson on hypnosis.* Ernest. L. Rossi (Ed.). New York: Irvington. [Book]

Haley, J. (1973). *Uncommon therapy: The psychiatric techniques of Milton Erickson.* New York: W.W. Norton and Company. [Book]

Kiewa, J. (1994). Self-control: The key to adventure? Towards a model of the adventure experience. *Women and Therapy, 15,* 3/4: 29-41.

Lang, N. C. (2003). From pre-social to social: Creating simulations of groupness with populations which lack the social competencies to generate group. Prelude to group formation. Paper presented at the 25th AASWG International Symposium. Boston. October 17, 2003.

Massion, A. O., J. Teas, J. R. Hebert, M. D. Wertheimer, and J. Kabat-Zinn (1995). Meditation, melatonin and breast/prostate cancer: Hypothesis and preliminary data. *Medical Hypotheses, 44* (1): 39-46.

McKenzie, D. C. (1998). Abreast in A Boat - a race against breast cancer. *Canadian Medical Association Journal,* 159: 376-8.

Powch, I. G. (1994). Wilderness therapy: What makes it empowering for women. *Women and Therapy, 15,* 3/4: 11-27.

Ryan, G. W. and H. R. Bernard (2000). Data management and analysis methods. In N. K. Denzin and Y. S. Lincoln (Eds.) *Handbook of qualitative research. Second edition.* Thousand Oaks: Sage Publications: 769-802.

Segar, M. L., V. L. Katch, R. S. Roth, A. Weinstein Garcia, T. I. Portner, S. G. Glickman, S. Haslanger, and E. G. Wilkins (1998). The effect of aerobic exercise on self-esteem and depressive and anxiety symptoms among breast cancer survivors. *Oncology Nursing Forum, 25* (1): 107-113.

Spiegel, D., J. R. Bloom, and I. D. Yalom (1981). Group support for metastatic cancer patients: A randomized prospective outcome study. *Archives of General Psychiatry, 38*: 527-533.

Spira, J. L. and G. M. Reed (2003). *Group psychotherapy for women with breast cancer.* Washington, DC: American Psychological Association. [Book]

Stanton, A. and G. Reed (2002). *The breast cancer notebook: The healing power of reflection.* Washington, DC: American Psychological Association. [Book]

Strauss, A. L. and J. Corbin (1998). *Basics of qualitative research: Techniques and procedures for developing grounded theory.* (Second edition) Thousand Oaks, CA: Sage. [Book]

Sunderland, C.C. (1997-98) Brief group therapy and the use of metaphor. *Groupwork, 10,* 2:126-141.

Wellisch, D. K., D. L. Wolcott, R. O. Pasnau, F. I. Fawzy, and J. Lansverk (1989). An evaluation of the psychosocial problems of the home-bound cancer patient: Relationship of patient adjustment to family problems. *Journal of Psychosocial Research, 7*: 55-76.

8
'SAVE' Students Against Violence at Emery
A whole school initiative:
A small group approach

Lynne Mitchell and Dianne Cullen

We know that the youth we work with experience violence in many aspects of their lives. These are not just the youth that display violent behaviours but also the silent unknown majority; the youth who watch and observe but who nevertheless experience violence by being caught up in the culture of their community.

Research produced by the City of Toronto Youth Safety Sub-Committee (2000), indicates incidents of violence, for both victims and youth offenders, statistically are at their highest during the school day during the school year. Reported incidents on school grounds have increased with 44% of youth victimization occurring between noon and 6:00 p.m. on school days. Youth are victims of violent crime significantly more than any other age groups. In the community in which we work 27.5% of youth, the highest proportion in the Toronto area, report feeling unsafe. Community agencies, the Toronto District School Board, and Emery Collegiate Institute came together to address this level of youth related violence. This collaborative venture resulted in the implementation of the Students Against Violence at Emery (SAVE) program that is funded by The Federal Department of Justice, Government of Canada, National Crime Prevention Centre. This program is based on a collaborative community model that was piloted at another community secondary school. It is tailored to meet the needs of the individual school and most importantly driven by student-defined goals and agendas.

In this paper we focus on the SAVE program's goals and objectives as they relate to the youth participants. These objectives are:

- To increase their understanding of the impact of violence in their lives;
- To raise awareness of and support for crime prevention among youth at the school;
- To build capacity in youth by providing them with the knowledge and skill to deal with violence among their peers.

Our program hypothesis, in order to achieve these goals, is that a small group experience can have a positive impact on youth who are at risk of violence. The program was developed on the assumption that if youth are given the opportunity to meet during the school day with professional group facilitators and discuss not only violence, but their other daily challenges, it could be effective in mitigating the impact of violence. In our paper we will explore working with youth and our community partners and how this program enables youth to discover a variety of options and choices that are available to them. Specifically, we will talk about the issues and findings that we find interesting, illuminating, challenging, and relevant to group practitioners.

Program overview

This collaborative program targeted approximately 200 grade 9 students in their first year of secondary school and was designed to eventually involve students at each grade level. Interactive dramatizations involving students in various scenarios dealing with violence were the first stage of the program. Once interest was generated in the topic of exploring violence, students were then invited to join an 8-week lunchtime group program where violence-related issues/concerns could be discussed in a small group setting. There were fall, winter and spring sessions that were grade and age specific. At the time this paper was written in 2003, there were 77 males and 81 females, for a total of 158 students who participated in the winter and spring sessions. Attendance was voluntary, pizza lunch was provided and students were credited with some community service hours that were required for graduation.

Community agencies contributed facilitators who were paired with partners from different agencies. This allowed facilitators with different group skills to work together, which proved to be a complementary arrangement. Facilitators were able to draw on each other's knowledge and experiences to enhance the group process and interactions with youth. It also allowed the youth to become acquainted with various community resources. Facilitator debriefing and consultation sessions were held weekly. Supervision meetings were held monthly. Yearly professional development workshops were also conducted. There was a project coordinator who handled all administrative, scheduling and school liaison functions.

The project was guided by a steering committee comprised of community partners, school administration and staff, and Toronto District School Board representatives.

Program design and development

In our experience working with youth in other programs, through student focus groups and student evaluations, the message to us was clear. In order for violence prevention programs to be relevant to both males and females, it would be important to deal with the violence that occurs in many facets of their lives. They articulated four main concerns:

- Relationship violence including male on male, female on female, male on female and female on male;
- Family violence;
- School violence;
- Community violence.

The program was designed on the premise that it would be voluntary and youth defined and driven. We believed that this approach would prove to be more immediately relevant to them than a directed curriculum.

We did not provide an agenda of topics that we felt needed to be covered in the area of violence prevention; instead, the youth were allowed to develop their own topics for discussion based on their personal experiences with violence and/or their thoughts and feelings about it. Often topics for discussion arose that were seemingly unrelated to violence, such as the marketing of CD's, interaction with school staff/administration, birth control and drugs. However, facilitating this type of open discussion contributed to the general feeling by youth that their thoughts and feelings were important and worth discussing and that they were capable of making relevant choices. It is interesting to note that although the students chose topics that may have seemed irrelevant at first to the topic, the discussions did in fact gravitate to violence and its prevention. Through this process of student driven agendas, the group discussions did manage to deal with the four main concerns previously articulated, i.e. relationship, family, school and community violence. The facilitator debriefing meetings held immediately after the group sessions confirmed that the topics discussed did address the four main areas of concern in a timely, relevant and appropriate manner.

Why small groups?

The group process provided an opportunity for youth to present their topics in an atmosphere of trust and safety. The sessions were time limited, closed after the first session and confidential both in terms of other students in the school and school staff/administration. These features contributed to a sense of cohesion and trust in the group.

A comfortable small group environment allowed the participants to personalize any information that would arise in the group in terms of relevance to their own lives. For example, if we discussed how to identify an abusive relationship, there was always the opportunity to make it personal to their relationships or applicable to the relationships they saw around them. Through group process and dynamics, we tried to provide an atmosphere of safety where this personalization process could occur. The value of the personalization process was reflected in one facilitator's observation drawn from the final evaluation, *'Allowing the students the opportunity to pick the topics contributed to the discussion; their personal experiences added to the success of the process.'*

Developmentally the group setting was appropriate in that it provided an environment where youth could discuss with their peers old, new and emerging values on violence. Having adult co-facilitators provided a role model that was non-judgmental, non-authoritative, and non–directive. The groups were largely co-ed which provided an opportunity for males and females to relate to each other as equals, to learn from each other and to respect gender differences relating to the topic of violence. The group program attracted roughly an equal number of males and females (see 'Update and Implications for the Future' below). We aimed to meet the needs of both genders by being comprehensive in the treatment of violence by not just dealing, for example, with male on female violence.

The group process, directed by the guidelines that the group participants developed themselves and facilitated by professionals, allowed the youth the opportunity to experience a different form of peer interaction that was respectful and supportive, while allowing them to be cognizant of differences. The group members represented many different cultures, and in some cases it was the first time that many of these diverse individuals had the opportunity to sit together, talk and get to know each other on a personal level. This in itself may help to reduce the potential for violence as youth begin to see members of different ethnic and cultural groups as peers. In this way, the group structure and process actually contributed to providing a model in the here and now that reflected the non-violent approaches that we were indirectly attempting to teach. By experiencing new behaviours and interactions in the group, youth could take these new skills into their communities and implement them in a way that was relevant to their own lives. Non-violent interventions were not theoretical but had actually been practiced in the group setting.

Does the collaborative co-leadership model work?

Having the two group facilitators coming from different community agencies provided a rich environment for the students involved in the group process. They had the opportunity to experience two adults who did not normally work together develop a method for interacting with each other and the group in a collaborative and respectful way. For the facilitators involved in the program the experience was positive even though the facilitation styles were different.

When facilitators were asked 'Did the agency collaboration model work?' they commented:

'Yes, pairing facilitators from different agencies and backgrounds built the strength of group facilitation and was very complimentary'
'Different facilitation styles provided good balance and learning opportunities for all involved'
'Good mix of approaches, ideas and backgrounds'.

Reflections on the program

The voluntary nature of the program

There was an ongoing concern among the staff and administration of the school that the youth who really needed the program, i.e.: those for whom negative behaviour was an ongoing problem, would not self-select and join the program. We wrestled with this concern in view of our belief that voluntary attendance and indeed making the program relevant so that students would want to participate were ingredients to its success. We were gratified to discover at the graduation ceremony for the 'SAVE' program that the school staff who attended observed that the students that they would have hand picked as needing the program had voluntarily attended. The school administration advised that the word amongst the students was that the program was worthy of attending and it became socially acceptable to participate in the program. Comments from the students' evaluations indicated they wanted to become involved because the skills learned in the program had helped them to cope better with violence in their lives. The increased participation in the program pointed to its voluntary nature being an important and successful ingredient.

Curriculum based vs. group directed agendas

In a violence prevention group it could be argued that there are certain topics that should be presented by the facilitators for group discussion, such as how to identify abusive relationships; social skills for conflict resolution; the relationship between drugs, gangs and violence; consequences and ramifications of violence; and reporting of violent activities. The 'SAVE' program was specifically non-directive and based on the premise that the participants would put forth appropriate, relevant topics if given the opportunity. The facilitators found that the students did indeed choose topics that were both appropriate and relevant and included all the issues that might have been discussed in a curriculum-based program. When asked about their expectations for the program, one student responded '*I thought that the leaders would talk about violence and ways to prevent it. Instead I was surprised that we got to talk about what we wanted to.*'

The facilitators also experienced the positive aspect of facilitating rather than directing the discussion. They did not feel that the group was out of their control or meandering aimlessly through irrelevant topics. One facilitator reflected these views by stating:

'It is always best when the students lead the group. It helps them make the issues of anti-violence relevant to their lives and gives them the experience of making a group work.'

Facilitators' role

The facilitators tried to model a positive way for adults to interact with youth. They were non-confrontational and shared responsibility and power with the group participants. By doing so the group was able to assume ownership and responsibility for the functioning of the group and for an individual member's behaviour within the group. They were able to experience empathy and support for one another and work through violence related issues that might otherwise have been dealt with through the school's disciplinary system. The impact of this facilitation model also had a spill over into their interaction with other adults in the school. When asked in what way their behaviour had changed, students commented:

'Telling a teacher or adult what the problem is, is the best method in stopping violence'

'Instead of taking action in my hands I call for help and let the teachers and principal know the situation'.

Setting

The program experienced the challenges of facilitating process groups in a school-based setting. The facilitation style was such that adults shared power with the group members in a way that did not parallel the teacher/student relationship. Additionally, the structure of the group was different from the structure of the classroom in that group members established the goals and agenda and shared responsibility for the running of the group with other group members and the facilitators. We found that the skills learned were utilized effectively in other school settings and in situations involving students/students, students/teachers, and students/administration staff.

The facilitation model did seem to translate into youth seeing adults in a different light and in the role of the potential ally or helper in the area of violence as illustrated by the following student quote:

'I strongly believe and will always believe that violence is not the way, but now I realize that telling a teacher or adult what the problem is the best method in stopping violence.'

This facilitation model provided an opportunity for youth to develop skills that would be transferable to a classroom setting and as a life skill applicable in any environment.

Findings and conclusions

Evaluation tools

The grade 9 students who attended the drama presentations to generate interest in participating in the lunchtime groups completed evaluations of the impact of the presentation.

All students completed evaluation forms at the end of each eight-week session. The facilitators and school administration completed one evaluation form at the end of the school year.

The evaluation tools collected a combination of qualitative and quantitative data.

Findings

The evaluation conducted for the Emery SAVE project strongly indicated that the small group program model was effective in reaching students and building capacity within the community in the area of youth violence prevention.

Student survey results were highly encouraging:

- 100% indicated they had learned that violence does not solve problems
- 97% felt they had a better understanding of how to resolve conflict in non-violent ways
- 93% believed they had a better understanding of the effects of violence on people's lives
- 91% knew where to get more support or counseling
- 94% would like to continue meeting in the lunchtime groups next year
- Almost all students indicated their attitudes (90%) and behaviour (87%) to violence was different or somewhat different after participating in SAVE.

Students' comments further highlighted the program's effectiveness:

'I learned that violence does not solve problems'
'My behaviour has changed because now I know how problems begin (gossip)'
'I know how to identify violence before it escalates/prevent it from happening and how to solve something without violence'

When asked in what way their behaviour had changed, students indicated the following changes:

'Prior to joining SAVE, I didn't really despise people who fought with others or used abusive language even though I did none of those things myself. But I look at such people differently and stop and tell people I know to stop swearing.'

'Well I thought that if somebody ever harmed my family I would avenge them. I learned that I shouldn't do that and just let justice take its course.' 'I used to get so hot when something bad happens against me or to people I care about but now instead of taking action in my hands, I call for help like let a teacher, or principal, know the situation.'

'I learned that it is OK to let others express themselves in appropriate ways and that it is important for us to accept others' differences of race or whatever because no two people are the same.'

Update and implications for the future

At this point in the program (winter 2005), there are far more students expressing an interest in attending than can be accommodated. The popularity of the program continues to point to the success of its voluntary nature.

The concerns expressed by the youth have not changed over the four-year period. Students still choose to discuss violence in their lives relating to the family, relationships, community and school.

Currently there are more males than females signing up for the program. In another school where this program was also conducted, a similar trend emerged whereby after several years, more males than females participated. Further research is required to determine why this is happening.

Unfortunately, there is no mechanism in place or funding available to track individual students and thereby evaluate the long-term effects of participating in the program.

The program results and our research have shown that this is an effective violence prevention model to be used at the secondary school level.

Due to the collaborative nature of the program, it is continuing with the support of community agencies and the school without assistance from outside funding sources. However, because of its collaborative nature, this violence prevention model can only continue in the future with the combined support of the Toronto District School Board, Emery Collegiate Institute and their community partners.

References

Azima, F., and Richmond L. Eds. (1989) *Adolescent Group Psychotherapy*, International Universities Press Inc.

Berkovitz, I., Lessons From Violence in Schools, *Journal of Child and Adolescent Group Therapy* , Volume 9, (June 1999)

Bowlings, S., Zimmerman, T.S., Daniels, K. 'Empower'; A Feminist Consciousness-Raising Curriculum for Adolescent Women, *Journal of Child and Adolescent Group Therapy*, Volume 10, (March 2000)

Letendre, J., A Group Empowerment Model with Alienated Middle Class Eighth Grade Boys, *Journal of Child and Adolescent Group Therapy*, Volume 9, (September 1999)

MacLennan, B., Violence in the Schools; A Commentary, Summer 1999, *Journal of Child and Adolescent Group Therapy*, Volume 9, Number 2, (June 1999)

Metcalf, L., (1995), *Counseling Toward Solutions*, The Centre For Applied Research in Education, New York

Peeks, A., Conducting a Social Skills Group with Latina Adolescents, *Journal of Child and Adolescent Group Therapy*, Volume 9, Number 3, (September 1999)

Rose, S., (1998), *Group Work With Children and Adolescents: Prevention and Intervention in School and Community Systems*, Sage Publications

Schewe, P., (2002), *Preventing Violence in Relationships*, Washington, American Psychological Association

Youth Safety Subcommittee, City of Toronto, *Youth Crime Statistics Report*, (March 2000)

Wolfe, D., Wekerle, C., Scott, K., (1995), *Alternatives to Violence, Empowering Youth to Develop Healthy Relationships*, Sage Publications

9
Group work with refugee children in a multicultural bereavement program[1]

David Prichard

Introduction

In the spring of 2003 I completed an intensive training program at a center for grieving children and became a group facilitator for a multicultural program for refugee children experiencing traumatic grief. The multicultural program is a peer-support group program, and is based on the premise that participants may have lost not only family members through war, but may have been exposed to combat situations themselves. Further, many refugees are grieving the loss of their homeland as well as threats to their cultural identity. The program currently provides services to over forty children from eight countries.

This chapter has four areas of focus. First it presents a brief overview of the literature on trauma, grief, and refugees. Second, it describes the multicultural group process and discusses the use of artwork and other expressive forms of intervention when working with traumatized refugee children in bereavement groups. Third, it examines the secondary impact of this work on children and on the group facilitators. Finally, implications for group workers involved with this population are presented.

Review of the literature

According to the 1951 United Nations Convention Relating to the Status of Refugees, a refugee is a person who, 'owing to a well-founded fear of being persecuted for reasons of race, religion, nationality, membership in a particular social group, or political opinion, is outside the country of his nationality, and is unable to or, owing to such fear, is unwilling to avail himself of the protection of that country.' While some refugees relocate within their country of origin, most leave their homelands behind. Though leaving one's country of origin as a refugee may create a sense of safety and protection, it may also represent a tremendous loss and be a source of symptoms of traumatic stress. There is a substantial literature on the correlation between trauma and refugee status (including Boehnlein & Kinzie, 1995; Jaranson et al., 2004; Mollica et al., 1993). Very little, however, has been written on the trauma experienced by refugees stemming from having to leave their homelands.

What the literature reveals, is an active debate between those that want to link trauma and bereavement (Brewin, Dalgeish & Joseph, 1996; Hobfoll, 1991; Lifton, 1998) and those that believe that trauma and bereavement are distinct constructs that must be addressed separately for the person to recover, suggesting that one may mask the other (Lindy et al., 1983; Pynoos & Nader, 1988; van der Hart, Brown & Turco, 1990).

Green (2000) provides an excellent overview on the topic of traumatic loss, defined as loss that occurs suddenly and under violent circumstances. There is an overlap between trauma and death. The loss of protection through the experience of death of an attachment and the loss of a sense of safety through trauma both disrupts one's sense of being protected, and even the possibility of protection, perhaps forever (Green, 2000). Stroebe & Stroebe (1993) suggest a distinction between non-traumatic and traumatic death. If a person experiences a non-traumatic death, both day to day as well as routine coping resources may be interrupted while schemas about the world involving trust, safety, and so forth may not be interrupted. In the case of traumatic death, where the loss is sudden or violent, or traumatic such as rape or assault, the disruption of beliefs may be more profound, including a radical shift in perception of the world as a safe place to the world as an unsafe place (Janoff-Bulman, 1992). Green (2000) suggests a further difference that distinguishes trauma and grief is the direct assault to the life and body that constitutes a trauma, as compared with the more indirect experience of losing a person to whom one is psychologically attached.

The relationship between trauma and bereavement among refugee children became less a theoretical exercise and more real to me as I became a group facilitator for children in a multicultural group at a center for grieving children. My experiences highlighted for me the need for further training on group work with traumatized refugee children experiencing grief and loss.

Multicultural refugee bereavement group training

The multicultural program is one component of comprehensive bereavement services offered at a center for grieving children. Services at the center are almost entirely based on group work. Programs that have evolved and been established over the past 15 years include life threatening illness groups, bereavement support groups for children, adolescents and adults, motherless daughters support groups, and multicultural peer-support groups for children.

Prior to meeting with any consumers, it is required that group facilitators for all of the groups offered at the center attend 20 hours of training on bereavement and group facilitation. Trainees meet once a night for several months and each night includes a didactic/experiential component followed by an hour-long group facilitated by two trainees and supervised by a staff member. Presentation topics included: spirituality, refugee bereavement, living with loss, group facilitation, externalizing grief, expressive arts and grief, stages of human development, experiencing the loss of a child, a sibling, a parent, others.

The core of the training is participation in bereavement groups in which participants explore their own issues around loss and grief, in some ways mirroring the bereavement group aspect of what participants experience at the Center. This component helps participants to internalize the concepts being presented, and to identify and work on their own experiences of dying, death, grief and loss. One of the strengths of this model is that it allows potential group facilitators to experience what it is like to be a member of a bereavement group and to work at recognizing potential counter-transference that could arise in working with others on their grief issues. The groups meet weekly over a period of several months. The experience is intensely personal, at times profound and poignant, at times tearful and sad, and at times joyous and uplifting. Each trainee has the opportunity to facilitate a group session and to receive feedback from a Center staff member and the group members.

Apart from a brief descriptive overview, there is no additional training for group workers that facilitating the multicultural bereavement groups for refugee children. There is also no discussion of the potential for secondary trauma of group workers. These are serious limitations to the training suggesting a lack of understanding of the specific needs of workers facilitating groups with traumatized refugee children.

Multicultural refugee bereavement

The multicultural groups meet one afternoon a week at the Center for one and a half hours directly after school ends. Transportation is provided by the school system. There is a maximum of eight children in each of four groups per group per day and each group is facilitated two group workers. Groups meet on one of two days each week and are composed of children between the ages of eight and thirteen. Guidance counselors in the school system refer children. Inclusion criteria are vague, but at the minimum the child must be enrolled in an elementary or middle school and in some way have a cultural identity associated with a country other than or in addition to the United States. Most of the children are refugees from countries including Somalia, Sudan, and Bosnia. There have also been children from Guatemala, Chile, Mexico, and Korea. A guidance counselor always accompanies the children to the Center and remains available on site throughout the afternoon.

The afternoon has three components. First there is the pre-group, in which group facilitators meet for one hour in a group facilitated by a staff person and a clinical consultant. The one and a half hour bereavement group follows this with the children. Finally, facilitators meet again for one hour in a post-group facilitated by the staff person and the clinical consultant. The purpose and process of a typical afternoon in the multicultural program is presented below.

Pre-Group

At the core of the processes in place for group facilitators to be effective group workers is the pre-group. This is a mandatory one-hour session that includes the eight group facilitators (two facilitators for each of the four groups), and a staff member and clinical consultant who co-facilitate the session. Once all participants are present, a candle is lit on the table around which couches and chairs are arrayed. The group starts with five minutes of silence providing a time for grounding, centering, and letting go of the stresses of the day. This process mirrors the opening of the adult bereavement groups at the Center. The remainder of the time is spent checking in and processing any individual and group distractions and stresses.

One facilitator, Goran, shares that his mother, still living in Bosnia, had taken a turn for the worse, and that she would likely die within the next few months. He does not know whether he will be able to see her before she dies. Another, Sharon, talks about her reaction to a particularly moving moment the previous week when a thirteen year old Somalian girl, Sufia, had broken down and cried. Sufia had lost her mother and father two years ago during a raid on her soldiers by soldiers. Beth is harried and announces that she will need to leave the group because she had taken a job that would present a time conflict. Ruth, an MSW intern, discusses her amazement about the work done by an eleven year old Bosnian girl who had lost her two brothers and her father in the war before fleeing with her mother to the United States. Jim shares that Sahra, a nine year old Somalian refugee, had done impressive work in the Volcano room the previous week. She had become quite angry and had beaten on the boxing bag, yelling in her native language, and ripping phone books. He said that her time in the room had seemed quite cathartic.

The pre-group ends with five minutes of silence. The facilitators gather in the main room and await the arrival of the children, who are provided transportation from their respective schools.

Group

This is my first group session and I am paired with Steve, a veteran facilitator who had been with this group for over two years. Our goal for the day is to finish the memory boxes that the children had made over the past two weeks. The boxes are simple, made of pine and open on the top, roughly the size of a cigar box. Materials such as paint, crepe paper, magic markers, yarn, ribbons, were available and the children had been instructed to decorate the boxes however they chose. The previous week they had been asked to bring in items that they would like to put in the box that remind them of the person(s) they have lost. The boxes are now completed, and some of the children had brought in some items from home and placed them in the box. Each now had the opportunity to speak about their boxes.

Yusuf, a Bosnian girl, has papered her box on the outside with pasted on magazine pictures of pairs of children, one boy and one girl. On the top of the box is a picture of a family of four, a mother, father, and a young girl and boy. Inside the box, she has constructed a small cardboard bed on which was laid a small figure with long red hair made of yarn. The walls inside are painted blue. At the foot of the bed is a mirror, a small piece of cardboard covered tightly with aluminum foil. On either side of the mirror lay a small yarn figure, representing Sara and her brother, Milan.

'When I lay in bed at night I remember Milan. When I look in the mirror I see him beside me .. I miss him all the time. I miss him reading me stories at bedtime'

Milan was shot and killed three years ago in Bosnia at the age of fifteen, a victim of ethnic cleansing

This week, Yusuf has added some coins from Bosnia, a picture of her brother in a soccer uniform, and another one of the two of them together posed in front of their home in their native land.

Hassan, an eleven year old from Somalia, has painted his box black on the outside. Inside the box, three walls are painted red and a fourth wall blue. On one red wall is painted a large black cross. Another red wall has a crudely drawn rifle with a bullet coming out of it. A third red wall has several bodies drawn prone and crumpled positions. The blue wall is filled with small crosses, depicting a cemetery, Hassan tells us, filled with his friends and family who have died. White clouds are drawn above the crosses. Crosses of family members are painted blue; others are brown. There are six blue crosses.

'My father was killed first, then my two older brothers,' Hassan explains. *'My sister was an accident. I escaped because I was seven and was hiding with my mother and sister. Both my father's brothers were killed. This happened on one night four years ago. The men had rifles and made all the men and boys leave.'*

Inside the box, near the crosses, Hassan has placed a piece of wood. *'This is from a tree in my village. I brought it with me from Somalia, and kept it in my pocket. It is a tree my brothers and I played on as children.'*

The group is silent for a moment, until Nahla, a nine year old from Sudan, speaks up. She holds her box forward. It is covered in magazine pictures of animals; inside the walls are pasted with flowers and more pictures of animals.

'My family came here two years ago. We were farmers and I miss the animals of my home,' she explained, with a heavy accent. *'We live in a small apartment here. It is crowded and I miss my friends, especially Thani, who is still in Sudan. We liked to play outside. I miss the rest of my family, especially my grandmother and grandfather, because we can't visit them anymore, and I miss the stories they tell.'*

Though she is shy and speaks softly, her grief is clear. Her loss has many dimensions and levels.

The other children present and describe their boxes. Each story is unique and varied, some sad and despondent, others wistful and happy at recalled memories and recollections. I am awed by the depth of the loss expressed and equally impressed by the resiliency and courage of the children who have witnessed and experienced extraordinary life events.

Our sharing of the memory boxes complete, we take a snack break. Within minutes the room was full of pillows flying through the air, and all of us engage in a full blown pillow fight. There was laughing, running, tackling, and general chaos, not unusual in a group of children (or adults) releasing a great deal of physical and emotional energy. We decide to take another ten minutes during which time three children continued to wrestle on the large over-stuffed pillows lining the base of one wall, two others engage in a game of Stratego, and two start working on their collages, our next activity. Biar, a ten-year-old refugee from the Dinka tribe in Sudan sits quietly in a corner reading a book.

There is a knock at the door and Andy informs me that it is our week for the volcano room. The volcano room, also referred to as the hurricane room, the tornado room and the energy room, is a relatively new addition to the Center. It has emerged as a favorite activity among the children and serves as an adjunct to their group work. The walls are padded as is the door, and inside is hung a boxing bag. The floor of the room is littered with soft bataka bats, foam balls, stuffed animals and other objects safe for expressing emotions. There is a life-sized human doll, soft and made of cotton, propped against one wall. There is great demand for the room, and as only one child is allowed in at a time, with two facilitators, each child is allowed only ten minutes.

Khalid has requested time in the room, and I escort him down the hall with Victor. Victor has been coordinating the volcano room for over a year, and it is his job to facilitate the experience, assist in the process, and provide safety.

We take off our shoes and step inside. Khalid does not await instruction.

> *'I'm really angry today,'* he stated without preamble. *'I just feel like kicking.'*
> *'Do you know what you want to kick?'* Andy asks, following Khalid's gaze to the body bag.
> *'Can we use the bag again?'* It is often selected as Khalid's outlet for emotional release.
> Nathan moves into place behind the bag and Khalid quickly starts kicking and punching the bag. After a few moments, Andy starts to offer a few prompts.
> *'What are you kicking?' 'Let it out ...', 'come on, you can kick harder than that', 'what are you angry at ...', 'who are you angry at ....'*
> Interspersed among the prompts, Khalid's verbalizations include: *'Why did you die?' 'I hate you', 'I'm angry at you for leaving'.*

Khalid's energy seems bottomless and it escalates until culminating in a howl *'Don't leave me/I need you'.* At this, Khalid finally crumples to the floor in a heap, sobbing, exhausted, sweat intermingling with the tears on his face. His anger and frustration gives way to tears of profound grief at the tremendous losses he has experienced.

After sitting for a few minutes, Andy gently checks in with Khalid. Khalid speaks of how much he misses his father and his brother, both of whom had been murdered just over a year ago during the ethnic cleansing in Somalia. I am honored and awed by the cathartic work that Ahmed has done. His arm around my shoulder, Khalid and I walk quietly and slowly down the hall to back to our group. No words need to be spoken.

Our group finishes the session by cleaning up from our days activities, playing a CD that a participant has brought with them, three girls dancing and the one girl and three boys wrestling, David sitting quietly by himself and reading.

Post-Group

The group facilitators meet again with the staff member and the clinical consultant to process their groups and also to address any secondary issues that may have arisen for them, particularly in regards to their own experiences of loss and grief. The process and purpose of the group is similar to pre-group, though the focus is more on immediate processing of the group with the children and clearing ourselves for re-entry to our other world and lives away from the center.

During the check in time, each group worker has the opportunity to process reactions to their bereavement group. The stated goal of this time is for individual sharing; it is not a time for commenting on the reactions of others. Sometimes sharing is light and seemingly not connected to loss and grief, other times reactions are strong and the emotional triggers seem clear.

Suzanne reflected on the collages that three girls in her group produced from the stacks of magazines available for cutting and pasting. All three girls produced collages that show many girls with blond hair and fair skin. In each, the emphasis seems to be American culture characterized by faired-skinned blond haired girls. Two of the girls are from Somalia and have extremely dark skin; the third is from Bosnia and has skin with a dark olive tone.

I shared my experience with Khalid in the volcano room and spoke of the completion of the memory boxes. I was struck particularly with the resiliency of the children and their ability to move forward despite such incredible adversity. I was also struck by the connection I felt toward a Korean girl and her expressions of grief around the death of her father and the loss she felt toward her native country. I have a sister adopted from Korea, and we know little of her family of origin. My sister was abandoned at an orphanage in the early 1960's during the height of the Korean War. I recalled her struggle during adolescence with her racial and national origins, and how at that time she rejected her American name, Jennifer, and adopted her Korean name Hae Ja Joon.

Goran, shares that a new group member is from a town in Bosnia near where he himself was raised. He has learned from the child that the village that he knew as a child has been abandoned, much of it razed. He expresses anger at the ethnic cleansing, the death and the loss of so many of his friends and family, and the loss of his childhood village and home. Goran's voice softens and lowers as he goes on, gradually giving way to silence and tears which course gently down his cheeks.

The group ends with five minutes of silence and participants transition as best as they can out of the multicultural group experience and back into the other activities of their day.

Secondary trauma of group members

There is increasing concern about the impact of trauma-related narratives on other group members. Dyregrov (1997) cautions group workers from including members who vary widely in their exposure to traumatic events. 'If there are persons within a group who have been severely exposed to traumatic stimuli, while others were removed from such impressions, you run the risk of having them listen to the detailed description of those who were in close proximity to horror' (p. 600).

Children and are at risk for developing secondary traumatic stress reactions as a result of their exposure to traumatic sensory images. Refugee children are from many countries and their exposure to traumatic events is as varied as the countries from whence they come. Participants in the multicultural program may include the following:

1. a Korean boy who had moved to the United States with his mother when he was an infant, and whose brother had recently died of leukemia;
2. a Cambodian boy whose father recently died of cancer;
3. a Somalian girl who had fled a the village where generations of her family had lived and who witnessed the brutal deaths of her father and two brothers by ethnic cleansers;
4. a Bosnian boy whose father and uncle had died in the ethnic cleansing of his village;

5. another Somalian girl whose grandfather had recently died;
6. a Sudanese boy who after witnessing the brutal deaths of several family members, including his brother, father and an uncle, had been forced as a child soldier to eat organs of dead enemy

Clearly, there exists the potential for children to be traumatized by even portions of the narratives that emerge in the telling of the deaths of loved ones. A very real concern exists that less traumatized children may be exposed to severely traumatic imagery and thus be prone to secondary trauma reactions even as they are struggling to cope with their own traumatic experiences. Currently there is no mechanism in place at the Center to protect less traumatized children from the more severely traumatized, which is of concern to this writer. Multicultural programs need to be highly cautious as they consider group composition in bereavement groups and how to deal with the traumatic imagery that, in some cases, may be integrally interwoven with the narrative, art and play work done by the children in the course of the bereavement process.

Secondary trauma of group facilitators

There is also concern about the impact of exposure to traumatic events on group facilitators. Herman (1992) suggests that secondary stress reactions can be considered inevitable among helping professionals and paraprofessionals as they react to exposure to trauma survivors' terrifying, horrifying, and shocking images; strong, chaotic affect; and intrusive traumatic memories. Figley (1993) defines secondary traumatic stress as natural consequent behaviors and emotions resulting from knowing about a traumatizing event experienced by a significant other; the normal stress reactions resulting from helping or wanting to help a traumatized or suffering person.

There is evidence that workers secondarily exposed to traumatic events may experience traumatic stress symptoms (Figley, 1995; Herman, 1992; Pearlman, 1995; Prichard, 1997). There is a paucity of research on the more specific secondary impact on helpers working with traumatized, bereaved refugee children.

It became clear to me very early on in my facilitation of the multicultural groups that group workers were at risk for traumatization due to their exposure to the narratives of sometimes extremely disturbing narratives of the children. A particular narrative comes to mind. Ali, a thirteen-year-old boy from Somalia had been told by his mother to flee the village after men with guns descended it upon. Ali, then eleven, had fled and wandered for weeks before being captured and forced to fight. His narrative is compelling. He relates having been forced to watch the heart and liver be cut from a dead man. These organs were then cooked and the abducted child soldiers (himself included) were then forced to eat the cooked human organs. He watched as other child soldiers were ordered to shoot and kill another runaway child or be shot. He had himself shot and killed one child soldier and numerous adults, alleged to be soldiers. Ali eventually escaped and had wandered for several weeks before getting out of the country and into a refugee camp. Ultimately reunited with his mother, he has never heard the fate of his father or two brothers, who, he is convinced, are dead.

The graphic details of the narrative were not shared with the other children in the group; they were shared with a group worker, who later experienced sleeplessness, nightmares, and intrusive thoughts. Nothing in the training at the center had prepared him for the horror of some of the narratives to which he was exposed. There is great need in the literature on the secondary trauma associated with working with traumatized refugee children, individually and in groups.

Summary

Grief is a very complicated phenomenon, especially when working in groups with child refugees. Add to this the traumatic experiences to which some of the children have been exposed and group work with this population becomes harder still. Complicating these groups even further is the fact many multicultural program rely primarily on volunteer and student interns to facilitate groups that may be composed of an extremely divergent group of children, from many cultures with levels of trauma ranging from none to severe. The potential for sharing and growth is great as is the potential for secondary trauma among group participants.

In a similar vein, while there is training for group facilitators to examine their own experiences with dying, death, loss and grief, there is a complete lack of training on *trauma* and no acknowledgement that the hearing of traumatic narratives within the bereavement groups could have a secondary *traumatic* impact on the facilitators. There was also no access to the intake information of the participants by group facilitators and therefore no pre-group preparation as to the loss or the trauma experienced by group members. This lack of prior knowledge creates a strong potential for facilitators to be taken totally by surprise and, along with group members, to be exposed to sensory detail that is intense and horrific. Group facilitators lack the information they could use to help group members from being unnecessarily exposed to traumatic sensory imagery.

There is a need for bereavement programs to integrate training on trauma and posttraumatic stress into their training curriculum and into their services and for policies to be developed concerning refugee bereavement group composition, relative to trauma experience. Further research needs to be conducted on the secondary trauma risk for group participants and facilitators involved in bereavement groups for traumatized refugee children.

Note

1. Identifying data of facilitators and group participants has been modified to respect privacy and to maintain confidentiality. This chapter is dedicated to refugee children of war torn countries who have lost a loved one through the trauma of war or who have lost a national identity due the imposition of village, national and/or global politics, about which they often have little interest or say

References

Boehnlein, J. and Kinzie, J. (1995). *Transcultural Psychiatric Research Review,* 32, 223-252.

Brewin, C., Dagleish, T. and Joseph, S. (1996). A dual representation theory of posttraumatic stress disorder. *Psychological Review, 103,* 670-686.

Figley, C. (1995). *Compassion fatigue: Coping with secondary traumatic stress disorder in those who treat the traumatized.* New York: Brunner/Mazel.

Green, B. (2000). Traumatic loss: Conceptual and empirical links between trauma and bereavement. *Journal of Personal and Interpersonal Loss,* 5(1), 1-17

Hobfoll, S. (1991). Traumatic stress: A theory based on rapid loss of resources. *Anxiety Research, 4,* 187-197.

Herman, J. (1992). *Trauma and Recovery.* New York: Basic Books

Janoff-Bulman, R. (1992). Shattered assumptions: Toward a new psychology of trauma. New York: Free Press.

Jaranson, J., Butcher, J., Johnson, D., Robertson, C., Savik, K., Westermeyer, J. ,and Spring, M, (2004). Somali and Oromo Refugees: Correlates of Torture and Trauma History, *American Journal of Public Health, 94*(4), 591-599.

Lifton, R. (1988). Understanding the traumatized self: Imagery, symbolization, and transformation. In J. P. Wilson, Z. Harel & B. Kahana (Eds.*), Human adaptation to extreme stress: From the Holocaust to Vietnam,* (pp.7-31). New York: Plenum.

Lindy, J. Green, B. and Titchener, J. (1983). Psychotherapy with survivors of the Beverly Hills Supper Club fire. *American Journal of Psychotherapy, 37,* 593-610.

Mollica, R., et al. (1993). The effect of trauma and confinement on functional health and mental health status of Cambodians living in Thailand – Cambodian border camps. *Journal of the American Medical Association, 270,* 581-586.

Pearlman, L. and Saakvitne, K. (1995). Treating therapists with vicarious traumatization and secondary traumatic stress disorders. In C. Figley (Ed.), *Compassion fatigue: Coping with secondary traumatic stress disorder in those who treat the traumatize*d. New York: Brunner/Mazel.

Prichard, D. (in press). Critical Incident Stress and Secondary Trauma: An Analysis of Group Process, *Group Work.*

Prichard, D. (1997). The primary and secondary impact of critical incident stress among police officers and their domestic partners. Unpublished doctoral dissertation. Richmond, VA: Virginia Commonwealth

University,

Pynoss, R.and Nader, K. (1988). Psychological first aid and treatment approach to children exposed to community violence: Research implication. *Journal of Traumatic Stress, 1,* 445-473.

Stroebe, W, and Stroebe, M. (1993). Determinants of adjustment to bereavement in younger widows and widowers. In C.M. Stroebe, W. Stroebe, and R.O. Hansson (Eds.), *Handbook of bereavement: Theory, research, and intervention,* (pp.208-226). New York: Cambridge University Press.

Trainman, E. (1992). *Fire in my Heart, Ice in my Veins: A Journal for teenagers experiencing a loss.* Omaha, NE: Centering Corporation.

United Nations. (1951). *Convention relating to the status of refugees.* Geneva, Switzerland: UN.

Van der Hart, O., Brown, P. and Turco, R. (1990). Hypnotherapy for traumatic grief: Janetian and modern approaches integrated. *American Journal of Clinical Hypnosis, 32,* 263-271.

10

Creating connections among disadvantaged youth

Toward participation in policy
development for social change

Nancy E. Sullivan and E. Michelle Sullivan

Introduction: Natural groups

In the professionally sophisticated groupwork practice which currently abounds, it is typically found that social workers apply their knowledge and skills with formed groups, i.e., groups whose members are selected and/or invited from a client pool with some predetermined sense of purposes and focus. However, community-based practice with natural groups is well established in the annals that document our social work with groups heritage (Brown, 1991; Coyle, 1959/1980; Heap, 1979; Klein, 1972; Mullender and Ward, 1991; Northen, 1988; and Wilson and Ryland, 1949/1981). These groups are 'associations of people who select one another, perhaps because of interest, similar characteristics, or physical proximity' (Brown, 1991, p. 242). They are people 'spontaneously drawn together by forces of the environment and mutual attraction' (Wilson and Ryland, 1949/1981, p. 3), 'whose own aims and norms are already clarified and accepted by their members by when the worker enters the group' (Heap, 1979, p. 22). Examples of natural groups are friendship and family groups, and groups that emerge within a workplace, long-term care facility, or housing complex.

Characteristics of natural groups

These include:

1. pre-existing acquaintanceships or relationships among members, possibly of long duration;
2. acknowledgement and acceptance of members as belonging, even if not explicitly articulated;
3. a core of shared customs, culture, norms, and/or worldview, tacitly or overtly expressed, including means and styles of communication;
4. cohesion already present due to the members' ability to identify with one another; and
5. existing potential for, and perhaps lived experience of, mutual support and collective strength.

Inherent in natural groups are traits that may confront the worker with particular challenges in a practice situation:

1. The cohesion already existing through the naturally occurring ties among the members, and to which the worker is an outsider, may so continuously reinforce and solidify their attitudes and behaviours that change efforts are impeded.
2. The environmental context of the group within which the members belong, such as a school or neighbourhood, may exert so strong an influence that other new influences cannot be introduced.
3. Due to the immersion in common among all the members in the shared environmental context, it may be difficult to distinguish individual or interpersonal situation-specific problems from members' 'response to social disorganization within [that environment]' (Brown, 1991, p. 241).

The focus of this paper is a natural group of adolescents, ages 16 to 18, who have participated recently in a project funded by Health Canada Atlantic Region on engagement of marginalized, at-risk youth in policy development at the community level. Having introduced the chapter with an overview of the nature of natural groups as they may be encountered in social work practice, the next section will provide some background and description of the project within which the group functioned. Aspects of the groupwork related to the tasks of the project then are outlined according to the characterization of a natural group.

Finally will come some conclusions with regard to the group process and the 'products' of the endeavour. Benefits for the young people as a result of their participation in the project will be discussed as well as implications for practice with natural groups in the movement toward increased community level citizen participation.

Background and description of the project

The project within which the group participated has its origins in the philosophical compatibility of several Canadian provincial and national initiatives focused on inter-related health policy, social capital, youth, and poverty alleviation. These programs each contribute to a fabric intended to increase the level of citizen engagement in participatory democracy in Canada. Certain federal programs such as Health Canada's broadly defined determinants of health and the National Child Benefit Program aimed at the reduction of youth poverty, have set the stage for provincial programs such as the Community Youth Network (CYN), which is the context for this project. Another major federally supported organization, the Social Sciences and Humanities Research Council, provided a platform from which this project could be launched by awarding a Community University Research Alliance (CURA) grant to a team including the co-authors of this paper. The Values Added CURA states, as one of its central purposes, to examine 'the voluntary community-based sector's role in building community capacity, encouraging socially inclusive citizen engagement, and fostering a climate for growth and development.'

A central focus of our project is the enhancement of skills and abilities of youth in the areas of understanding and interpreting social policy. This stems from the premise that the depth and breadth of the social capital base in the rural and remote home communities of the project target population will be improved by their gaining an increased appreciation of the implications of social policy at local, regional, provincial and national levels.

The overarching purpose of the project is to enhance participation by excluded youth in social policy development, monitoring, and modification, with immediate and sustainable application through a community empowerment model based on principles of participatory democracy. The specific objectives include assisting excluded youth in identifying policy issues that impact on their lives by enhancing their skills and capacity to expand their understanding about social policy, to explore policy alternatives and policy development work, to gain some experience in applying their skills as policy contributors; and to increase knowledge regarding the process by which engagement in policy development happens.

The target population for this project was young people already participating in the Community Youth Network (CYN), organized in Hub Sites across the Province of Newfoundland and Labrador. The CYN is designed to improve the life chances of youth living in poverty and experiencing other marginalizing conditions. It seeks to improve the educational, employment, community/social and communication/technology environments in which our project youth reside. In the Province of Newfoundland and Labrador the life chances of young people often are substantially compromised by factors which include low population density spread over a large geographic area, high rates of youth poverty, high rates of unemployment, literacy difficulties, and infrastructure and educational limitations related to the extent to which the population lives in rural and remote parts of the province.

The specific focus of this paper is a group of young people associated with the St. John's CYN Hub Site and is referred to as the Reference Group. The phases of the project for the Reference Group have included initial engaging in, and making a commitment to, the work of the project; meeting with the project coordinator to design workshop content and activities, participating in the delivery of the workshops at four sites, and taking part in identification of the learning experienced. The workshop sites were situated in remote and/or rural areas of the province, with the exception of one workshop that was delivered at an urban alternative education facility.

At each workshop site the participants organized themselves by choosing seats at separate tables (4-6 per table), each designated as a 'Tribe' in a Survivor Island Game. This game format was an original idea contributed by the Reference Group and given its youth friendly nature was very well received by workshop participants. All workshop activities took place within this structure.

There were two streams of activity. The first was the Survivor Island Game which required tribe members to respond to interpersonal issues within their imaginary tribal communities. An example of this was an exercise where each tribe was presented with the possibility that members of their island community exhibited challenging personality traits such as 'always angry' or 'always complaining', and was asked to identify the considerations necessary for the community to live co-operatively. The second was the Mapping Activity which introduced the youth to concepts of social policy by inviting them to examine policies that are present in their lives within five spheres: the personal, the home environment, the school and social environment, the local community, and the provincial/national context. This was accomplished through the use of life size poster outlines of the human body drawn on brown paper. In this exercise tribe members wrote real time examples of policy relevant to the sphere on the poster and then taped it to the wall of the room where a representative of each tribe presented the material to the whole group. The workshop, which spanned two days, was punctuated by various team building and energizing activities, many of which were at the suggestion of the Reference Group. Two of these were a Jello Eating Contest, and a 'Mini Survivor Game' in which each workshop participant was asked to complete an inventory of his/her own community resources.

Characterizing features of this natural group

1. Inter-relationships among the members

The seven young people who functioned as the Reference Group for the project are interconnected through longstanding ties in the local community, some because of the close proximity of their homes, and others due to attending the same schools. They did not meet as a group in the usual way in social work practice. Although there were many 'sessions' for preparing the workshop materials, they were not held at regular weekly times but rather as needed, and all seven members rarely attended the same meeting. This happened partly because of the school, employment, family, and social activities in their lives, and, to a great extent, because of the task specific nature of the work of the project and the individual skills and abilities required at different times, such as artistic abilities.

It was clear in the early exploratory meetings, that in addition to the natural connections among the Reference Group members, each was unique in his/her own right. It was observed that interaction among these young people often resembled that seen in families: sometimes conflictual as in the manner of sibling dynamics, often supportive, and always loyal to defend against outside threats.

The inter-relating among the group members often was in the form of parallel dyads, the equilibrium among them frequently disrupted by the intrusion of aspects of their separate personal lives. For example, concerns regarding the health and well-being of parents would elicit worry and stress that was carried into the group context. While all acknowledged the common focus of the project, and identified strongly with one another, these young people remained a 'grouping' or 'collectivity' of previously existing relationships, never evolving to a fully formed 'group' as an inclusive entitative social form (Lang, 1986).

2. Shared base of culture and norms

Members of the Reference Group engaged in this project were, without exception, experiencing two or more of the life challenges previously mentioned as characteristics of the CYN target population. Most of the members of the group were residing in social housing communities, and thus were subject to the classic negative stereotypes held by the wider community. Although the communities from which the Reference Group was drawn indeed are over-represented in the provincial demographics for high risk indicators. It is worthy of note that each community has made significant progress in working toward an improved quality of life for its citizens, in particular, the youth. An example is the establishment of vibrant community centres as a base for advocacy, social action, and service delivery. Our Reference Group members were secure in the context of their own home communities, however, their membership in these communities continued to set them apart in potentially socially isolating ways within the larger social environment of the city.

Although the Reference Group members and the workshop participants share the social and demographic characterizing traits of the CYN target population, the Reference Group members' functioning seemed to be further compromised by their social disadvantages, particularly in the early workshops. Being asked to integrate and participate in new settings and activities seemed to remove the safety associated with familiarity, and resulted in such behaviours as inability to attend, restlessness, and inappropriate comments. These behaviours at times compromised their ability to accomplish their co-presenter function.

While some settling in and acquaintance making would be expected for the Reference Group and the participants at the start of the workshop in each new site, there were noticeable differences between the two cohorts. For example, when workshop content and format shifted from social to substantive activity, it often triggered banter, disengagement from the workshop focus, and an apparent need for the comfort of smoke breaks among Reference Group members. When the workshop was presented at an alternative education site with somewhat more mature participants, those individuals initially were intolerant of the Reference Group members' disruptive behaviours. These differences were reconciled in short order, and the Reference Group members and the workshop participants began to establish social ties. By lunchtime on the second day, members of both groups enjoyed playing hackey sack together before returning for the afternoon session of the workshop.

3. Mutual support in relation to task achievement

Among these young people as a natural group, mutual support was observed frequently in the interaction as a naturally integral characteristic of the pre-existing alliances between certain youth. Two friendship pairs in particular served as anchors around which much of the mutual support activity revolved, often positively and sometimes negatively. Mutual support was observed when youth were faced with social and/or task expectations outside the frame of reference of their previous experience.

As the date of the first workshop approached, time lines were tight. Consequently, some of the detailed material preparation was required on the eve of the first day. Following a long, stressful road trip, the youth were asked to colour some handouts for the following day. This request generated displeasure in one young person, which in turn released an avalanche of negative response from other group members. Resolution of this situation was reached after the group had finished venting, by the encouraging intervention of one of the group members. Supported in turn by the project coordinator, this particular young woman relied on her strong positive influence upon the youth to engage them in understanding that the colouring task was important for the success of the workshop and for the enjoyment of the participants.

As in this first example, there were several incidents that encouraged the emergence of natural leadership among the youth throughout the course of the project. Another group member contributed her organizational skills to marshal 10 people through meal time. This young woman drew upon her family background in the catering industry first by making the suggestion and then proceeding to take the breakfast orders the night before to assure that the group was relaxed and well-fed in ample time for the morning workshop session to begin. The positive response of the group to this initiative was a good indication of mutual support. This practice was so well received that it was employed during subsequent workshop trips with the credit for the origin of the plan reinforced on each occasion.

A third young woman was seen to blossom over the duration of the project in terms of her leadership abilities, willingness to assume responsibility, and support of her peers. This support was observed in her direct and indirect actions. She gave verbal encouragement to those who were hesitant to speak in public, recognized the need to give helpful direction and assistance to the presenters, and often jumped in to fill a gap. Her leadership was non-threatening and served to generate and reinforce a group spirit of mutuality.

Numerous additional illustrations of mutual support emerged during the project. One young man's exceptional spelling ability was recognized and regularly relied upon. At the beginning of the fourth workshop, his increased social confidence enabled him to move from the table where his tribe was seated to join a 'tribe' of youth from the local site. He continued there comfortably for the duration of the workshop. It is likely that this young person's natural tendency toward social engagement was released through the spirit of mutual aid that characterized the group throughout its time together.

Another young man's obvious grasp of the conceptual basis of the workshop content similarly was encouraged to flourish to the point that, at the fourth workshop, he took the lead in presenting core material with confidence and capability. Many times during the project mutual support was evident among the members as many of them coped with personal crises intruding on their lives outside the group and from incidents occurring within it.

Ironically, on several occasions during the project, mutual support was present in a potentially harmful form. During an overnight stopover in an unfamiliar town on the return trip from the first workshop, the youth lobbied for the freedom to spend unsupervised time. It was agreed that one hour would be reasonable and they were driven to a shopping mall where local youth were gathered. When they returned to the hotel it was clear that they had not only engaged with the local youth but also had accepted a ride through the town in cars with young men they had just met.

Debriefing of this incident was initiated immediately. In response, the four young women presented a united front and objected to the possibility that their behaviour had been unsafe. They angrily stated that they were being treated like children. They were unable to perceive the risk and liability concerns of the workers and were insistent upon further communication with these male youth who were hovering near the hotel. Following heated negotiation they agreed to remain in the hotel for the night and did so, despite their continued protestation as a group.

This incident resurfaced and clearly was still unresolved when attempts were made several weeks later to meet for detailed preparation for another road trip. The young women expressed their resentment vehemently. They perceived the workers to be criticizing them on a personal level implying that they were not 'good enough' and needed to change. The response again was very raw and the youth, in an expression of solidarity, left the room. The tasks intended for the work session were abandoned as the powerful dynamic of mutual support dramatically engulfed the situation.

It bears note that as potentially beneficial and nurturing as mutual support can be and has been for these young people, two caveats may be added. The first is the possibility that, given the pre-existing relationships among natural group members, mutual support may take on the function of a negative contagion effect and significantly predetermine the disposition of the group against growth, personal change, and, in this project, accomplishment of tasks. Secondly, however positive and sustaining of group members mutual support can be, it alone cannot compensate fully for personal challenges such as intellectual limitations and compromised ability to attend and focus on content, situational challenges related to family circumstances and other relationships within the community, and environmental challenges regarding availability of resources.

4. Role of the project workers as group workers

Just as this Reference Group holds characteristics of a natural group, rather than one formed in social work practice, so too has the role of the project workers been distinctively different from that of a group worker with a group in an agency setting. The adult members of the project team included the project coordinator, the coordinator of a separate but related project, and two of three authors of the project. (The third had been centrally instrumental in designing the project but had relocated to another province for most of the activity phase of the project, returning for the final workshop trip.)

The project coordinator, at the point of hiring, was given three primary areas of responsibility; namely, to engage participants of CYN St. John's as a Reference Group for the project, to work with the Reference Group to design and prepare the workshops, and to undertake the logistics of trip planning and workshop arrangements at the sites. From the start, the project coordinator understood her role to be that of a youth worker, helping the young people sift through the chaos of their lives and relating with them in ways that would earn their respect and trust. This was essentially a relationship building task and she effectively connected with them individually, in dyads, and collectively as a group. Her intervention was extremely valuable at this stage of the project in assuring that the youth felt sufficient ownership that they would commit themselves to participating in the workshop planning and maintain their involvement throughout the presentation phase.

From the outset the central motivator for the youth to participate in the project was the incentive of the opportunity for travel within the province, an experience that was new for many of them. The coordinator's willingness to recognize and work with this priority was a very powerful tool in the engagement process. The statement 'we all want to go on the trips' became the unifying goal for youth, and the engagement goal for the coordinator. Understandably, given their age and stage of development, fun was a powerful motivating force which they associated with taking trips and was particularly relevant in engaging them in rapport building and energizing activities for the workshop. They saw these 'fun activities' as fundamental to a successful workshop.

The social policy content aspects of the project were developed as a collaborative effort between the project coordinator and the coordinator of the other, related project, the primary purpose of which was social policy education and application within the not-for-profit sector. The nature of the other project generated content that was readily transferable to the design and substance of the workshop. In the execution of her role with this project, the other coordinator participated in the organization and delivery of all but the final workshop and as such was a full member of the team. Her focus was on the content and delivery of the workshop, in contrast to the role of our project coordinator who focused on the interactional process among the Reference Group members. Although both made necessary contributions, tensions developed around role clarity, personality, and the perception of the other project coordinator as an outsider. She was regarded as an intruder in the close relationships already formed between the Reference Group and the project coordinator, and in the tasks of the workshop development for which they had begun to feel ownership.

The depth of the relationship between Reference Group members and the project coordinator was evident in her consistent naming of them as 'my youth'. Their strong reciprocal relationships resulted in her joining with them in their natural group culture. In allying herself so closely with the young people, the coordinator contributed to their sense of empowerment and their tendency toward self-protection against outside influences. This was reflected when the coordinator and Reference Group members were challenged to address the need to learn new skills required for workshop presentation. It appeared that she viewed this instruction to be invasive, implying criticism of the existing abilities of the youth, and beyond the parameters of her role and that of the project.

Conclusions

Participation in the project provided this natural group's members with a multitude of opportunities for personal and social development and enrichment. Their experiences included the development of a sense of ownership in the CYN which they came to describe as 'our CYN', this ownership facilitated significantly by the strength of the relationship between them and the project coordinator. Beyond the central focus of executing the project, the availability of the project coordinator to model strong positive problem solving skills, to be available and non-judgmental and to support the youth, was an immediate and important bonus to their involvement. This likely was a key factor in their continued engagement in the project, which in turn expanded the horizons of positive influence available to them.

This positive impact includes: the enrichment of exposure to communities beyond group members' natural environment, the expansion of their personal networks through the establishment of relationships with peers in other parts of the province, the learning that came from living the reality of travel by road and air to remote destinations, the personal anxiety of separation from family members which was a new experience for many, the experience of value and behavioural expectations that fell outside their usual frame of reference, exposure to knowledge related to the issues that affect the daily lives of their peers who live in rural and remote communities, the contribution to general skill banks and competence that came with developing and presenting the workshop, the growth in understanding of the social policy concepts that emerged for most during the course of the project, the generalized positive impact on self esteem and personal confidence that came from involvement in the various aspects of the project, and the affirmation of evolving skills that was reinforced further by their engagement in the project.

We have come to know this natural group as having characteristics that are consistent with those identified in the literature. The opportunities provided by this project allowed for these young people to extend the parameters of their longstanding relationships and, in the process, to derive multiple personal, social, and educational benefits. Through their involvement, the young people built upon a pre-existing level of connectedness without impeding the closeness of the more intense friendships which were maintained throughout the project. All the young people expressed a sense of belonging as members of the project team and were clear about their sense of ownership. While it is true that this natural group was sometimes resistant to perceived incursions upon their culture, the cohesiveness, the familiarity and security inherent in their sense of belonging allowed them to support one another and to grow. Ultimately, the success of the project in achieving its stated goals rested upon the strength of spirit brought to the task by the cohesiveness, loyalty, and tenacity of the group.

Implications for practice with groups in social work include the potential for positive group process and useful outcomes with natural groups. As the current trend toward the international evolution of participatory democracies continues to evolve, the engagement of natural groups in community citizen participation and decision-making becomes an increasingly relevant issue. Those who practice social group work may find themselves in an environment where a strong understanding of natural groups and the competencies to engage them successfully will be critically needed by civil society. This knowledge and skill base is strategically poised and directly applicable for making a relevant contribution.

Acknowledgement

This project owes a debt of gratitude to the primary funder, Health Canada Atlantic Region; and partners Community Youth Network, St. John's Region; The Brother TI Murphy Center; Provincial Department of Youth and Post Secondary Education, Government of Newfoundland and Labrador; and Dr. JoAnne Zamparo at the Lakehead School of Social Work, Thunder Bay Ontario for her contribution to the project design, implementation and analysis. The project was also affiliated with the Values Added, Community University Research Alliance (CURA), funded by the Social Sciences and Humanities Research Council (SSHRC).

References

Coyle, G. L. (1959/1980). Some basic assumptions about social group work. In A. S. Alissi (Ed.), *Perspectives on social group work practice: A book of readings* (pp. 36-51). New York: The Free Press.

Brown, L. (1991) *Groups for growth and change.* New York: Longman.

Heap, K. (1979). *Process and action in work with groups: The preconditions for treatment and growth.* Oxford: Pergamon Press.

Klein, A. (1972). *Effective groupwork: An introduction to principle and method.* New York: Association Press.

Lang, N. C. (1986). Social work practice in small social forms: Identifying collectivity. *Social Work with Groups,* 9(4), 7-32.

Mullender, A., and Ward, D. (1991). *Self-directed groupwork: Users take action for empowerment.* London: Whiting & Birch.

Northen, H. (1988). *Social work with groups* (2nd ed.). New York: Columbia University Press.

Wilson, G., and Ryland, G. (1949/1981). *Social group work practice: The creative use of the social process.* Hebron, Connecticut: Practitioner's Press.

Index

groups and feminism movement 34
group stages 18–22
Group, The (journal) 2

H

Health Canada 131
health insurance 70

I

identification 69
Intelligence Quotient 62
involuntary client 8, 16

K

Kaiser, Clara 1
Konopka, Gisela 2

L

Lindemann, Eduard 76
literature
  and diversity education 49
literature groups 47–60
lymphedema 88

M

McGill Domestic Abuse Clinic 9
Medicaid 70
memory boxes 120
mentally retarded and developmentally disabled (MRDD) adults 61–73
  definitions 62
metaphor 98
misogynistic culture 30, 42
Motivational interviewing 15
multicultural group process 115, 117
mutual aid 68, 136

N

National Association for the Study of Group Work 2
National Association of Social Workers 3
National Conference on Social Work (NCSW) 2
National Jewish Welfare Board, 2

www.ingramcontent.com/pod-product-compliance
Lightning Source LLC
Chambersburg PA
CBHW062034270326
41929CB00014B/2428